SHAPERS AND POLISHERS

TEACHERS AS STORYTELLERS

Betty Rosen

Collins Educational

An imprint of HarperCollinsPublishers

The boy ... enjoyed the one about the lamp that fulfilled wishes and about flying carpets. Surprised, he asked Ursula if all that was true and she answered him that it was, that many years ago gypsies had brought magic lamps and flying mats to Macondo.

"What's happening," she sighed, "is that the world is slowly coming to an end and those things don't come here any more."

One Hundred Years of Solitude
Gabriel Garcia Marquez

Material is added or subtracted by chance and circumstance, but to survive a story must have the approval of audiences, who thus keep it and its teller on the rails. Millions over the years have thus supplied the shaping while the tellers supply the polish.

The Past We Share
E L Ranelagh

This book is dedicated to all those children and teachers who have believed in stories and recreated them for themselves in my presence.

First published in 1991 by Mary Glasgow Publications Ltd.

This edition published 1993 by
Collins Educational
An imprint of HarperCollins*Publishers*
77–85 Fulham Palace Road
London W6 8JB

Printed in Great Britain by St. Edmundsbury Press, Suffolk.

ISBN 0 00 314366 X

CONTENTS

Part 1 NEW TERRAIN

Chapter 1 Introduction.. 3
Chapter 2 The three-year-olds meet Abiyoyo........................... 10
Chapter 3 Abiyoyo: thinking about it afterwards 18
Chapter 4 Into the primary classroom 23
Chapter 5 Is my tale too frightening? 29
Chapter 6 Five-year-olds and The Giant over the Mountain.............. 38
Chapter 7 A Welsh Giant for adolescents and adults....................... 46
Chapter 8 Exploring personal experience 52
Chapter 9 Autobiographical storytelling:
          The School Cap by David Horner 58
          Grass by George Murphy 62
          Mine's called a Totee by Rosalind Watson 65

Part 2 TEACHERS' WORKSHOPS

Chapter 1 Irish tales, Oisin, and the realm of mermaids 68
Chapter 2 The many faces of retelling stories............................ 77
Chapter 3 N A T E: gaining confidence 99
Chapter 4 N A T E: a participant's viewpoint by Jean Dunning 112
Chapter 5 Conclusion 121

Part 3 THE TALES

Twelve stories to read or tell in class which are either mentioned in the text or have a relevance to some section of it.

Introduction 127
1 The Land Where No One Ever Dies 132
2 Death and Sweet William by Judith Baresel 137
3 The Thieving Monkeys 146
4 The Singing Drum 149
5 The Mice and the Fircones 153
6 The Bald, Warty Giant by Chris Stelling 156
7 The Giant Injection by Carol A. Cooke 158
8 Chaim and the Chrane by Harold Rosen 160
9 I Remember Ponty 166
10 Usheen 171
11 The Fisherman and the Mermaid 174
12 The Fisherman and the Mermaid by Jean Dunning 180

Bibliography 188

ACKNOWLEDGEMENTS

First and foremost I am grateful for the encouragement and support given me by my husband, Harold, during the writing, shaping and polishing of my present story — and all the rest of the time too. The following people have all contributed, some directly by allowing me to use their spoken or written words here, or by inspiring me with a tale or two of their own for me to retell; some indirectly by just being enthusiastic towards my efforts as a teacher/storyteller or as an author of this kind of book: Rosalind Watson, Jean Dunning, David Horner, George Murphy, Judith Baresel, Chris Stelling, Lynda Jones, Carol Cooke, Harold Rosen, John Davey, John Foggin, Michael Rosen, Alastair West, Pat Lowe, Helen Campbell, Jane Grell, Jean Leonard, Heather Sharpe, 'Tuup', Adrian Peetoom, Nick Hutchins, members of the London Narrative Group and all those people, old and young, who have welcomed me into their classrooms, colleges and teachers' centres.

Part 1 NEW TERRAIN

Chapter 1
INTRODUCTION

This book is about exposing the creative resources which teachers have within them. I have come to the writing of it even though an author's hat sits as something of a novelty on my head. I write because I have a new and important tale to tell. It is about teachers and the stories of teachers.

During my final few years as a full-time teacher, I became a storyteller in my own classroom to sufficiently good effect to want to write up the whole experience. I described my own practices and my pupils' responses in the form of tellings and retellings of tales old and new. Once the book was written and published — *And None of it was Nonsense* — I found this third professional category of 'Author', tacked on to the other two. It was then that various individuals, both friends and strangers, invited me to come into their classrooms — pre-school, primary and secondary — to tell stories to their pupils. English advisers, lecturers in education, and the kingpins of teacher organisations of one sort or another began asking me to come to talk about, and organise workshops around, the activities I had described in my book. Best of all, perhaps, were stints in particular schools for up to ten days at a stretch, working alongside classroom teachers and their pupils. I also worked several times with adult EFL students and our activities focused on stories.

In the course of this work I learnt some more about my own voice as a storyteller and a very great deal about the real voices of my colleagues in the profession. This is what my second venture into authorship is about. Let me recap and reflect a bit first before I get down to the job in hand.

Just over three years ago I stopped being a teacher because my services were no longer required by my employers. The school where I had

3

learned to tell and receive stories is now razed to the ground. The developers, who purchased the Victorian building and promised, a 'gentlemen's agreement', to keep its basic structure intact, sneaked out at the dead of night — literally — with the bulldozers. By morning, the whole site was ready for clearance, and the building of another Yuppiesville in Thatcherdom. So much for my teaching career. So much, perhaps, for education as I have always understood it to be …

The sight of that broken shell of a building sounded a hollow note in my interior. I am ashamed to admit that the symbolism dwindled to a little knot of self-pity. It is a stark jump from being a teacher, a 'senior' one at that (in the days before grading), to being a nobody — especially if one happens to be, let us say, in one's middle years. No one made a great fuss about it; common as muck these days, early retirement. I would be bound to find things to fill my time. I would go to cookery classes — I'd always needed to, and that's a fact; I'd learn Welsh, if I could find a tutor, cheap; I'd go swimming with my grown-up daughters once a week at least in Park Pool on 'ladies only' nights. It would certainly be nice to see a little more of them than I did when they lived at home with their senior teacher mum. Air fares will take some saving to visit my son in New Zealand. Best of all, I would have the chance to write up some of my classroom experiences if I could manage to do so in a form which invites readers. If not? Well, there was always supply teaching — which would be in demand as a teacher shortage was undoubtedly in the offing. With the onset of centrally dictated curricula, a multiplication of bureaucratic chores and, last but not least, testing (of children and teachers alike) for the sake of testing, plenty of teachers would be glad to leave the profession and few would be eager to join it. But I did want to write up those experiences.

As it turned out, writing the book was very pleasurable, as were the consequences of doing so which provided me with the meat of this next one. By accident, you might say. Until I became a 'pensioner', writing a book was simply not on my agenda any more than it's on yours, if you are like most people. Especially if you happen to be a classroom teacher. I do know people who write books in the normal way of things. I know one such person very well indeed.

I'd been living with a senior academic for a long time before the 'academic' became 'citizen'. Sociologists tell us about such transitions so perhaps I should not have been so surprised — appalled would be a better word — to hear him on one occasion considering the possibility that retirement might mean landing up on the shelf along with the books he'd authored, never to be taken down again, even for dusting. I'm sure they don't all feel that, the learned ones. Some produce instant autobiographies. Some have got so used to their own brand of literacy that they are immediately motivated by a compulsive urge to pass on to posterity all the wisdom of their hindsight. Not this one, however. In spite of efforts by family and friends to prise a *chef d'œuvre* out of him, nothing has emerged as yet. Retirement, did I say? He wrote papers for lectures, journals books; he received more invitations from educational establishments than he could possibly accept, and still does; he read and tutored and seminared as busily as in his pre-retirement state. But there is still no sign of the Masterpiece.

The most promising hope to date arose as a result of the arrival on our doorstep of a determined Canadian publisher who had come all the way from Toronto with one sole purpose to get a book out of Harold Rosen. He was bedded down on the instant, jet lagged, and proceeded for all of ten days thereafter to be fed and watered under our roof while working on the Professor Emeritus. It inspired one morning's endeavours which may or may not move on to better things. This was a ransack of the house for any item bearing witness to my husband's penmanship. Harold dug and delved. The anxiety of it all left him in a state of frantic disarray, no less than that which he created within yawning cupboards, box files, filing cabinets, cardboard boxes, the cellar, the attic and upon every horizontal surface of the home. During the other nine and a half days there was a much more comfortable questing into the nooks and crannies of my husband's past life which he enjoyed exploring with the Canadian. What will come of it remains to be seen, with any luck.

As a classroom teacher, I too have my life's records. To exclude for a moment the surprise of that bookful (*And None of it was Nonsense*, MGP 1988), what's in print is not hard to find as it is contained upstairs in one small drawer in one small cupboard in our smallest bedroom, known to us as the Amstrad room. Amongst these items I have even kept a letter to the *South Wales Voice* written when I was sixteen about seal spotting off Rhossili sands and a translation, executed at about the same age, of *Le Jaguar* by Leconte de Lisle which appeared in *Y Darren*, Ystalyfera Grammar School's magazine, not long after the Head of English had kindly provided me with its very last word — *expunges*, to rhyme with

Into the dark depths the victim plunges.

There's more recording scattered about in my own handwriting or two-fingered typescript, but most of that kind of thing has been filed in the bin year after year. And no one has saved my letters for publication. (I once knew someone who thought that everything — but everything — he composed should be saved for posterity; if my husband had a bit more of that attitude in him the kind of rummaging I referred to earlier would make the house look less like a training ground for robbers or MI5.) Once my 'senior' bit arrived, the services of school secretaries were applied to my more formal professional reflections and, though we have moved house since I left the chalkface, I still have the evidence. Reading it is not altogether rollicking fun.

The mass of them — my records — are in my head, just as yours are in yours. I ask you, do publishers cross the Atlantic to winkle them out of us? Do people so much as cross the street to demand a write-up of our life's work?

The fact is, people don't. This is because nobody knows about us. In the case of the man I am married to, it would be true to say that the Canadian and I are not alone in hoping for a major work to emerge from his powerful pen; he is known already, and rightly so. Rank and file teachers are not only not known but all too often are ignorantly maligned. Teachers' voices must be heard, however, even against all the odds and oddities of officialdom. Gone are the days when educational 'evidence' emanated from ivory-towered universities. The worst comes from politicians. The best arrives from teachers themselves, sometimes in collaboration with academic educationists, sometimes not. Even some of the most dictatorial of those who make rules for us concede that no pronouncements can be made from above to any effect unless they are fit to be validated by the experience of real teachers in real classrooms. And our voices are at their best telling stories, our own stories and stories we have made our own. These pages contain such testimony.

While most of us — 'us' being primary teachers, secondary English teachers, ESL teachers, support teachers and all such people concerned with language development — do not think of ourselves as writers; we spend chunks of our lives trying to turn others into writers with the aid of the 'writings of authors'. What an irony! Many teachers of art paint pictures, woodwork teachers will turn bowls or make furniture, teachers of dance show how to move to music and whoever heard of a music teacher who could not play an instrument or sing a note? These people are not practitioners of their craft in the professional sense that they earn their living from these activities, but their real strength is in their capacity to do as well as to teach. Few teachers of language, however, actually write — or even consciously talk — creatively, in the way that we expect our students to do. Thus we neither develop our own language as we could nor surprise ourselves by our own skills in manipulating words to creative ends.

I believe that teachers are a very talented lot without being tribally aware of it. In these dark days we hear more about our shortcomings from every Tom, Dick and Maggie who know all about what we should be up to in school because they themselves have been there, among the rows of desks, and have emerged to their own satisfaction. It is fashionable to denigrate teachers in the press and on television with disastrous consequences to the morale of those on the receiving end. No one talks these days about teachers' strengths.

It would be nice if one could command some superhuman power to bellow more loudly than the media about the real value of teachers. As it is, perhaps the only occasion any of us formally sets about blowing our own trumpet is in the course of filling in an application form for a job. After completing the obligatory list of arid facts — mere titles of stories which may never be told to the unnatural air hanging over the formal interview room — one is faced with composing the letter of application or filling in the section on the application form headed "Other points you wish to make" or words to that effect. It is this task which sets up the pen-chewing: what else is it about me — the overwhelming most of me — which hasn't been stated so far? What am I really like, at my best? What am I actually capable of?

There are magic beans for spilling here. How often I have wished for a magic *means* of spilling them. Even now when I am really desperate for truth to be revealed I catch myself hoping for divine intervention. I remember occasions during morning assembly at my old grammar school when we were wrathfully informed of some crime committed by an anonymous sinner somewhere in our midst, a sinner who was oh, so well protected by his opaque exterior! I hadn't done it but I blushed to think that the headmaster didn't know that. Perhaps he'd think I was the villain. Perhaps his eye would catch mine in a minute. I would stare in vain into the innocent faces of my peers for tell-tale signs while simultaneously trying to shed my portion of unwarranted corporate guilt. God's attention, I felt certain, would undoubtedly have been drawn to that hallowed hall by such an articulate expression of righteous indignation on the part of E D Lewis, Headmaster. Surely the

Good Lord could send forthwith an enormous digit through the ceiling which would point out the culprit precisely and let the rest of us off the hook? It was the same superstitious spirit which alerted me out of my torpor in history lessons upon hearing how Martin Luther hurled an inkpot into a corner of his study window because he saw the Devil peeping in at him; or how John Bunyan, on a damp country walk, did trust in the Lord and point at a wet patch on the track before him, saying, "Puddle, be thou dry!" By sixth form and university, it seemed to me that the likes of Shakespeare, the great novelists and the poets — study-worthy weavers of words — were more sacredly threaded to the Almighty than were the likes of Martin Luther. These were the ones with personal access to the Lord. How was I to know then that the divine is within us all and access must be found for it!

Until comparatively recently, whenever I found myself lost for words, particularly written ones, there would come upon me the superstitious notion that the perfect form of expression was actually hovering about within some abstract, invisible cloud just above my head, unattainable by me because I was not chosen as an Author in the Great Design of Things. Working on stories myself and working with teachers working on stories has put such frustrations into the realm of past fantasising. There is an infinite variety of ways of saying if only we get down to the job with confidence. In broader terms, there is an infinite variety of language content and practice within the classroom, but the only successful forms are those negotiated by teachers themselves out of their own experiences and talents. No higher authority exists which can substitute for this. Talent, like narrative, is not exclusive to the few but is all around us waiting to be released. Talent does not hover above at a distance but is within us. The magic that will shift it into the open is the magic of stories, from the everyday experiences of our own lives and from that corporate witness to the lives of those who occupied past cultures, which is the folk story.

It now seems a long time ago that I plucked up all my courage to close the book and tell a folk story in the classroom, as an activity peripheral to the real business of education. From there it progressed to the mainstream classroom at the heart of the learning process, even in upper secondary examination-dominated classrooms. That I have recorded in the shape of my pupils' creative responses to the wonder of story itself.

In this present venture I want to record how, as someone trained in secondary school teaching, I have extended my own capacities and insights by bringing stories to pre-secondary school children. I believe in myself now as a creator of stories, which is to recognise a new dimension of my personal and professional identity. But much more significant than this is to have discovered, through story workshops, amazing creative skills I could not have guessed at within my colleagues in the profession. I hope here to give something of the flavour of that discovery: its implications regarding the quality of the teaching profession and the massive potential which lies just below the surface.

Whatever demands on teachers' talents may be made by central government, the reality is that teachers have extraordinary powers to create their own plan of action. If at this time teachers do not take positive initiative there is no hope. Market values — false values — are being poured from above, displacing the human ones from an education system which simply will not survive without us. Such madness cannot last and we must have the confidence to make the shift ourselves, now. We do not deserve to submit to, and be demoralised by, that which is imposed upon us. We have all the necessary ability, imagination and energy to construct collectively the curriculum we teach. A central part of that collaboration is participation in experiences which are the same in kind as those we know from experience are right for our pupils — the reading, the listening and, particularly, the speaking and the writing. When that happens our own creative powers are liberated in ways which astonish us and everyone else. It is certainly that way with the making and telling of stories. Through them, perhaps the potential of humanity will be allowed back on the agenda: that, after all, is the only raw material we have in our professional lives!

At its simplest, my hope is that this book will turn many teachers into classroom storytellers, will strengthen the resolve of those who have already hesitantly made their first attempts, and, for those who are already paid-up members, will point to new possibilities.

Chapter 2
THE THREE-YEAR-OLDS MEET ABIYOYO

When it comes to sharing one's assets, family comes first, friends next and the rest last. Family these days can extend to all sorts of step-people, in-laws and ex-in-laws. My first encounter with *And None of it was Nonsense* in all its bound and picturesque glory came as a parcel of ten free copies which I was eager to flash about. One for me, one for my husband, one for each of my three children, one for my sister, one for my husband's sister, one for each of his grown-up sons, one for my friend — the ex-wife of his eldest ("my daughter-out-law" as he calls her), maybe one for the 90-year-old second husband of my late mother, one for Monica who is my closest friend, and one for Moishe and Rene — my closest London friends. The number of copies in the cardboard box didn't tally with the number of selected recipients. Thus began the seemingly endless purchase — yes, purchase — of further copy after copy. It still surprises me how many individuals expect me to give them one free. I forgive them because they know rather less than the little I know about authorship. They think there's money in it, which no doubt there is if your name happens to be Bruce Chatwin or Salman Rushdie, but not for us amateurs, even with a book which my publishers tell me is "doing quite well". I reckon my labours have paid something less than ninety pence an hour. Just think, round our way a visiting mender of washing machines demands a £40 call-out charge and may only stay five minutes.

Not that I mind the low pay. My real value, I tell myself, is as a teacher or, more topically, as a storyteller. That's where family and friends come in again. My daughter, Rosalind, when in possession of palpable proof of fame (if not fortune) in the shape of a real book with her mum's name on the cover, asked if I could come and tell stories at her pre-school centre in Holloway where she is employed as a child-care worker. Yes, I said, of course.

What presumption in that response! I am a fully trained, experienced secondary school English teacher, not at all equipped to cope with a quantity of tiny, noisy, scurrying things that are barely out of nappies. That's the rashness of putting the needs of family first. It's all of nineteen years since Rosalind, my youngest, began being little so I have forgotten the toddler wavelength.

Let me describe how I began to learn to tell stories to the very young.

I was as nervous as I had been on that first occasion of bookless storytelling in my secondary classroom, now almost forgotten. The story I finally chose was *Abiyoyo*, based on an African lullaby and folk story, retold by Pete Seeger and published by Hamish Hamilton in 1987. It is beautifully illustrated by Michael Hayes: I flirted with the idea of punctuating my telling with showing the pictures but I knew that would be cheating. No printed page must intrude upon the oral telling of a tale. Pictures must grow in the mind. It had to be, as before, just the storyteller and her audience.

Audience is hardly the right word. My style of telling up to that point depended upon fixing the listeners' attention at the outset and allowing the spell of the story to bind them into silent stillness to the very last word. With such listeners only the imagination is active. Anyone used to very young children, however, knows perfectly well that 'activity' among them means mobility of arms, legs, whole bodies, nearby objects and, above all, tongues, in addition to the mysterious invisible movements inside their heads. In my naivety I still clung to my faith in the mesmerising power of story.

Rosalind, with enviable assurance, marshalled them into a squirming clump on their miniature chairs. I sat myself down on a high stool with another one nearby for my handbag into which I began a self-conscious fumble: I didn't want them to know about the presence of a tape recorder which would, I hoped, help me to prevent a repetition of any follies that I might perpetrate should I venture a second time into the domain of the under-5s. It was hard to be efficient. I was reasonably certain I'd pressed the 'record' button but didn't stop to check. The longer I kept my eyes away from those little people, I guessed the more likely it was that they'd waft off, like so many dandelion seeds.

I had pressed the correct button. In those early days of my literary triumph I could hardly have known I would find that tape useful in telling a new set of readers about that afternoon's experience. But I can tell you, quite precisely. Here is as faithful a transcription as I can muster. I began …

Right …

Here's your hankie, Rosalind.

Oh, thanks, Losanne.

Oooooooooooh! There's worms on that! Ha ha!

(Thinks: there's worms on what ...?) *Right! Shall I tell you a story about a giant? You know, a great big giant man. Right. Now here we go.*

Now all my story happened in a little village a long way away in Africa.

I went on my holidays to Trinidad.

I went on my holidays to the hairdressers.

And there's a little boy in my story and his name is Yowi. Now Yowi is a very nice little boy but he's sometimes a bit naughty and the reason why he's a bit naughty is because sometimes his daddy is a bit naughty. And I'll tell you about his daddy. His daddy had got a magic stick called a zoop stick and when he waves his magic stick and ...

You're naughty boy! (Bellowed by a little round faced boy in green.)

... er ... and touched something with his magic stick, do you know what happened? It disappeared! So he could take his magic zoop stick and ...

You're ... naughty boy! (Same fellow as before.)

And touch this young man with the green jumper on and then — whoooop! He'd disappear. But he hasn't disappeared because I haven't got a magic zoop stick, have I?

Nooooo! Nooooo! (Many voices.)

Well this daddy ...

Noooo! (One voice.)

... had a magic zoop stick so sometimes somebody would be sitting down, just going to have their dinner, nice big plate of rice and peas, and he'd get his zoop stick and he'd touch the plate of food and — whooop! — it would be gone!

(Someone giggles. Says — whooop! Giggles again.)

And there'd be the somebody going to have their dinner, his mouth all watering, and where's the dinner?

All gone!

All gone! And another time he got his zoop stick and somebody was just going to drink a nice glass of mango juice, see, and he got his glass and he went to have a drink and this daddy touched the glass with his zoop stick and — whooop! — the glass disappeared and ALL THE MANGO JUICE WENT ALL DOWN HIS FRONT!

(Murmurings.)

And he was all wet! Ooooh! And all sticky!

(Giggles and laughter.)

And he didn't get a drink of mango juice at all! So you can see he was always playing tricks on people.

Now his little boy, Yowi, a bit older than you. Yowi, his little boy, the one thing he wanted more than anything else in the world was to be a famous pop singer with a guitar. He wanted to play a guitar in front of the cameras. You know, have you seen them on the television?

Yes .
Yes. Yes.
I've got a guitar.

You've got a guitar?

(Increasing hullabaloo of voices ...)
I've got one, too!
I've got a guitar
I have! I have! And me!

(One tot with big brown eyes and a lacery of little black plaits over her head leaps off her chair to tell my nostrils that SHE has a GUITAR. In no time the whole pack of them are round me in an intense, breathtaking swarm.

Frantic, I hear myself begging them to sit down and tempting them with the prospect of what might happen next in the story but my voice, closest to the tape recorder, sounds relatively much more convincing than it actually sounded to my 'audience'. Rosalind rallied the troops and eventually I found myself back to ...)

Right ...
Right then ...
This little boy ...
This little boy, he had a guitar, too.

(And the racket broke out all over again. To be honest, though Rosalind continued to do sterling work, there were all kinds of enthusiastic interruptions and sound effects from this point on until the story took a serious turn with the appearance of the promised giant. What's more, another little group from the next door room was let out into the play yard (I should think so, too. Best place for them.) shrieking and squealing over the trikes and scooters and climbing frames, to such an extent that the tape recording becomes something of a joke in spite of its proximity to the visiting storyteller.)

This little boy called Yowi, his nanna gave him a guitar. So he got the guitar and he started to play. But he hadn't learnt how to play properly, see, so when he started to play it went noing noing noing noing noing!

(Lots of laughter at my impersonation of a tuneless guitar)

What a horrible noise — but he didn't care, he just wanted to make sounds on the guitar, so he wandered round the village and all the way he went noing noing noing! on the guitar.

(Imagine the joinings in now — choruses, dirges, wailing walls — not to mention the laughter and a "Look at your hair! It's going all messy!")

'Course it is and so was Yowi's hair. And do you know what? In the afternoon, in the nursery school, when all the little children were ready for their nap and going to sleep, Yowi arrived just near the open window of the nursery and what do you think happened?

(If you ask a stupid question ... The children seemed to be enjoying the story immensely but not in a way I was used to. But then, it wasn't the kind of story I was used to telling, either. In fairness to that story I think I'll just transcribe the narrative itself for a while and let you imagine the audience participation.)

... So all the children woke up and started to cry. And that same evening, when the old folk came out for a nice little quiet chat together as the moon came up, there was Yowi creeping up behind them with his guitar. What a horrible noise he made!

Well, this went on day after day until the time came when everybody in the village said, "That's enough! We've had enough of your guitar," they said to Yowi, and they said to Yowi's daddy, "We've had enough of your zoop stick too. We can't put up with you and your tricks any more, making people's dinners disappear and making their drinks spill all down their fronts. You can't live with us any more; you'll have to live in a special little house just outside the village."

So Yowi and his daddy couldn't live in the village any more and they weren't allowed in at all and they lived all by themselves. And they lived by themselves for a long time. And while they were living by themselves, Yowi's daddy thought, I wish I could use my zoop stick to be good to people instead of playing tricks on them. And Yowi practised on his guitar and learnt to play good tunes on it which he was sure people would like.

Now one day, just when the sun was setting, just when the sun was going down, people were looking out of their houses watching the sun go down — it was lovely evening light when suddenly (in a whisper) *everything went very dark and when they looked up there was a big shape in front of the sun, blocking out the light.*

It was the giant, Abiyoyo.

(From whisper, crescendo to BIG VOICE.
And I gradually stood up.)

(Back to a whisper.)

Everybody said, "Hide! Hide! Lock your doors! Don't go out! Abiyoyo the giant is here!"

(Deep, dark voice.) *And Abiyoyo was there in front of the sun on the mountain side.*

(Some little giggles, infectious, at each Abiyoyo entry ...)

And Abiyoyo picked up a cow in his hand and (vivace!) *he-popped-it-in-his-mouth and ate it all up!*

15

And all the people screamed and cried, "Stay in your houses! Hide under the tables! Hide behind the door! Don't go out because Abiyoyo is there!"

(Deep fee-fi-fo-fum voice again.) *And Abiyoyo the big giant man came down the side of the mountain again and* (quick change to allegro) *he picked up another cow and shshshlurrp!* (move to a distinct allegro vivace) *he gobbled it right up quick as a flash! And* (whispers again) *Abiyoyo's hair was all dirty, full of spiders' webs. And Abiyoyo's hands were all dirty, all dirt under his big long nails. And Abiyoyo's feet smelt like cheese …*

(Big response from the children here!)

Abiyoyo was horrid! And the people were peeping round their curtains at him. Peeping out of their houses to see what Abiyoyo was doing.

And what (tones of sturm und drang) *did they see?*

They saw Yowi (confidential incredulity) *and his daddy, coming out of their little house.*

Go back! (ascent to tone of — controlled! — near hysteria) *"Yowi!" they called. "Go back, Yowi's daddy! Go back! Go back! Abiyoyo is there!"* (Followed by Big Dramatic Pause for the group experience of baited breath.)

Yowi and his daddy went right up to Abiyoyo. Abiyoyo said to himself, "There's a nice fat boy. I could eat him up in one bite! I could eat his daddy up in two bites!"

Yowi (Lente, lente! And down to whispers so quiet the tape recorder only just coped.) *began to play on his guitar but not making horrible sounds like he did before but he played and sang a nice tune.*

Ab -i-yo-yo   - Ab -i - yo -yo-   Ab -i - yo-yo-yo-yo - yo -yo - yo

Abiyoyo stopped and his eyes got big. Yowi played again.

(Repeat of song. This time some satisfied laughter and the murmurings of voices joining in. I invited them to join in with a third go. It was miraculous the way the children grasped the tune so fast. This is a delightful portion of the tape.)

Well, Abiyoyo was so pleased. He'd never heard anyone sing a song about him before. He thought it was lovely. And he listened again. (Couple more repeats of the chorus/song.) *Abiyoyo thought this was lovely and he began to dance on his great big smelly feet. And he was dancing and he was dancing and all the time he was dancing, Yowi was singing.*

(More singing. The children's involvement from the point of Abiyoyo's entry into the story had assisted the momentum of my telling and in no way got out of hand from my point of view. However, at this point I added a demonstration of Abiyoyo's style of dancing which — of course — everyone copied with glee. A certain chaos came again, I fear, but between us Rosalind and I managed to get them tuned into the denouement of the tale.)

I'll tell you what happened next. Abiyoyo danced and danced and danced and he got more and more tired, tired, tired and he started to go to sleep. Fast asleep. Asleep. And Yowi whispered to his daddy, "Now's the time. We will save the villagers from Abiyoyo." Yowi's daddy got the zoop stick — remember the zoop stick? (Several responses here, at length — but I wasn't afraid any more.) ... *That's right, so he came up on tip toe to where the giant was sleeping and he just touched the giant gently with the zoop stick on his head and — whooomph — Abiyoyo disappeared.*

And all the people of the village came running out. "Oh, thank you, Yowi. Thank you, Yowi's daddy! We'll never have a giant come and eat our cows or us again ..."

(Et cetera. General happy ending rejoicing. More singing. All over. Cup of tea needed.)

Chapter 3
ABIYOYO: THINKING ABOUT IT AFTERWARDS

Maybe I'm a bit more in touch with that age group than I thought; perhaps occasional contact with little neighbours and quantities of step-grandchildren is enough to do the trick. I didn't think so beforehand, however. Then I had felt very threatened by these tiny volatile strangers. I had already asked myself all those questions which any teacher, convinced of the value of telling stories to children but short on the confidence to try, has to face: which story should I choose? How should I tell it? Will I need pictures? Will I need props? How does the age of the children affect these matters? How well must I know them to make a success of it? How far should I go in acting the giddy goat? Dare I sing a song ...? Once in their presence my nervousness actually increased, and there was no release until that point in the story when Abiyoyo's appearance electrified them. Only then did I feel sufficiently controlled within myself to forget me and tune in to my listeners. It's the doing of these things that brings the answers to key questions. Anyone who wants can learn just as I did.

This was in a different league from engaging with secondary school pupils. In a nutshell, the difference between this occasion and any other storytelling session I had been through in the past was that it was dramatically more interactive among all those involved. It was an overtly communal event.

I am reminded of a time, over a decade ago, when I moved out of teaching secondary children and student teachers (both part-time jobs) to teaching 8-year-olds full-time as a conscious choice. It was an enormous culture shock but I learnt fast, perhaps because there was no acceptable alternative. The real transition was from working with people at a certain distance to being suddenly at close proximity, physically and metaphorically. And this is the parallel with the Abiyoyo event.

The 8-year-olds seemed to engulf me. They touched my brooch, held my hand, stroked the cloth of my skirt, all so unselfconsciously that it would have been hurtful to recoil. Each child had so much to tell me and such pathetic faith in trapping my undivided attention, in spite of the other five or ten individuals simultaneously behaving in exactly the same way. Once, while seated on my desk reading to the whole cluster of them, I became aware of a tickling sensation up my calf: Lenore had hold of the zip on my left boot and was slowly zipping and unzipping with her fingers while her ears dealt with the story. My initiation into the world of the primary school was both moving and utterly exhausting. And no free periods! I can remember doing deep-breathing relaxation exercises during the weekly television programme and the headmaster's assembly. Secondary teachers can all too easily pretend that their pupils are objects, vessels to be filled. The reception class teacher cannot escape the whole persons before her, especially when they have tantrums or wet their knickers.

Or worse, says Rosalind, to return to her charges. The story I had told them engulfed us all — orally, physically, visibly. In the days and weeks that followed, Abiyoyo became a household word in the nursery and joined the folklore of their common culture in a way that no other storybook in use had done up to that point. Eventually I bought them a copy of the book itself which immediately jumped to first favourite. Even now, many months after that visit, children will come up to Rosalind to sing, or demand, the Abiyoyo song and one of them frequently greets her with, "Ab — i — yo — yo — is — com — ing!" in the most *profundo basso* her four-year-old larynx can muster.

Much of this is because of the nature of the story itself (which I shall consider later) but at least as much was due to the fact that this was a telling, not a reading. The conversational face-to-face encounter with at the first half of this story invited verbal response. Unlike secondary pupils, these little ones instinctively articulate recollections stirred up in the course of being told a story. For example, Yowi's misbehaviour calls forth that severe "You're naughty boy!" from the child in the group most used to being on the receiving end of such accusations. Hence, too, the burst of guitar claimants, whether actual or just wishfully thinking. This is more likely to take place in the course of a chat than a reading. Continuous eye contact helped to hold their attention (for a good deal longer than during readings, so I was told later) and no anchoring book restrained physical responses to the story — either mine or theirs. As a storyteller I am persuaded that the stimulus of a direct audience, without the barrier of print between us, pushes the human voice to explore its limits and leaves one free for plenty of body language, all of which strengthens the impact of the story.

I have read this story to similarly small children so I can make comparisons. Towards the end of a New Year party we had for various neighbouring families, I found myself with four under-5s tucked round me on the sofa with *Abiyoyo* on my knee. (I lacked the courage to *tell* the story in front of the adults!) The moment I reached the end, "read it again" was the cry. This must have happened at least six times in succession — it certainly is a grand story! However, though I would be the last person to belittle the value of reading to children, I was conscious that this *Abiyoyo* was a more sober, so perhaps a more transitory, affair than at the nursery.

Even with such young children, I am sure that pictures in the imagination of the receiver of a told story have more impact than pictures in a storybook. This was most obvious at the point when Abiyoyo himself enters the story, causing a dramatic shift in tone. Everyday village activity and mischief suddenly give place to fearsome fantasy. As suddenly, Rosalind's little troupe were stilled and every eye wide. During the description of him, the laughter was different from what it had been in response to the tricks of Yowi and his father. It was that distinctively nervous kind when humour's legs are wobbly. I was conscious of the need to adapt, second by second, to that audience in order to keep the danger zone just out of reach of reality in their busy heads. The children at the party, on the other hand, missed out on something. Their first sight of Abiyoyo was almost clinical by comparison. They were simply curious about the pictures of the giant, commenting, almost objectively it seemed, on the various parts of him in the illustrations as though they were pieces of a jigsaw. Because my *telling* was orchestrated by the minutiae of their reactions, I think Rosalind's children got the best of both worlds: comfortable reassurance came warm on the heels of tingling excitement. They had more fun from the scenes they conjured in their heads.

Perhaps the experience took them a little further forward in the process of de-blurring the boundary between infant fantasy and fact. Useful indeed, if one considers that in these early years, though fairies may replace baby teeth under the pillow with pocket money, very different creatures lurk under the bed at night and in the far reaches of darkened rooms. Even benign old Father Christmas can inspire tears when made flesh in the department store. I remember once taking a class of 12-year-olds to present their puppet plays at a similar nursery centre in Wallsend. The infants, seated on the floor gazing up at the 'Punch and Judy' type staging, were quite delighted with Humpty Dumpty — woolly, rosy, cuddly — until he fell off the wall and landed at the feet of those in the front row, causing a burst of unstoppable terrified screams. Makebelieve had intruded upon them too rudely. But a storyteller can safely steer Abiyoyo out of monsterdom into merriment and on to the communal well being of village — and nursery — life.

As for what it did for me, the storyteller, in one fell swoop I had extended my range well beyond what I had come to recognise as 'my' kind of story told 'my' kind of way. In *And None of it was Nonsense* I described what this means: briefly, I like stories which have a strongly lyrical or reflective quality which I tell in a restrained, literary sort of way. Elsewhere, too, I have stressed the importance to a beginner storyteller of establishing one's own personal taste in choosing and telling stories. Here, because of my audience, I had incorporated a much wider range of 'voices', lots of dialogue, more body language and physical movement; I had sung a song, led the singing and the dance; and — great surprise to me — made them laugh a lot! I had in fact moved closer to certain Caribbean storytellers I know, though it happened by accident since I would not presume to emulate those whose oral culture was bread and butter to them from the beginning. I should add that this process might have been assisted by a certain convergence on my part with the Afro-Caribbean connections of most of the infant audience.

I must add a final word about the strength of the story itself, though much of this must surely be obvious. It has 'reality' value — there are real people in it with their chatter, their dinners, their cool drink, their guitar, their children's nursery and lots more like that in the text itself; there's the mischief of the chief actors. There are fear, rejection and punishment, too, but warmly resolved without question marks, not just at the end but gloriously in that moment when Abiyoyo smiles to hear, for the first time, a song someone has made up about himself. It has the wonder of fantasy in the magic wand and the giant figure. It has that ingredient so much loved by small children — repetition, but (to reveal an intolerance!) not the sort which can bore the adult teller cross-eyed in the throes of interminable identical sentences and dialogues. Here, the zoop stick and the tuneless guitar can work their way into any of an infinite variety of contexts while the children can enjoy the fun of anticipating the familiar consequences.

It is a lovely tale. I heard it told by Jane Grell, a storyteller based in Waltham Forest, who brought this story alive for me in the first place. Hers was a much better telling than mine — she was herself reared on a diet of village storytellers in a small island in the West Indies. What's more, she had with her at her own storytelling a real guitar which she knows how to use. Which reminds me: on future storytelling occasions at Rosalind's centre I made a point of bringing objects, artifacts and items of clothing to help the stories along, things which could be felt and explored by the children. Little ones in particular relish the physical, the tangible: a guitar and a 'magic wand' to assist that tale would have helped them focus upon the story. Unlike book illustrations, which are essentially *interpretive*, such items are merely an extension of gesture — like the brushing of 'mango juice' off one's 'wet' front, or fingering the blank place where the 'rice and peas' had been. Having said that, I should add that many more storytelling occasions since have taught me that small children, too, can become absorbed by a quiet, thought-provoking tale which has no physical frills attached.

Even so, my storytelling initiation into the world of the very young was a far cry from the class of teenage boys in my past, immobilised from first to last by Orpheus' mythical lute and his insubstantial Eurydice.

Chapter 4
INTO THE PRIMARY CLASSROOM

Rosalind's function on that first occasion had to be that of mum-protector in a situation where I felt myself to be on show, like a stage performer. In a 'real' classroom I see myself and the teacher as co-workers: I am there in the role of collaborator in ongoing learning activities. My next partner in narrative conspiracy did not have to have this spelt out in advance as has been the case quite often since, for she was an old friend who shared my brand of professionalism.

The occasion was significant in two simultaneous ways: first, it set me seriously thinking about the whole question of the suitability of particular stories for particular age groups and, second, I found myself capable of a new kind of responsiveness to my listeners' reactions — an adaptation on my part which was both spontaneous and creative. This is how it happened.

My storytelling took place within walking distance of home but just as far from the experience of my old professional haunts as Rosalind's nursery was. Up a few streets, along the alley between the houses, down lots of steps in the region of the green pathway that is the disused railway line, and into the playground. Circumnavigate the sandpit and the climbing frame, a quick glance towards the secluded shrubbery bit under the sycamores and mountain ash (can this really be North London?) and I'm at the main door. Big WELCOME signs in many languages; bright posters; a patch of poems about spiders — Italic and Bold — each with its edge decorated with felt-tipped cobwebbing; a ring of red mushroom stools round a revolving bookcase as high as my waist; an exotic fish tank enclosing neon slithers which dart between swathes of green lacery; and everywhere, many, many pupils' paintings, too many for me to absorb in my search for people. Round the corner and here is a bustle of children with clipboards and pencils. There, in a carpeted recess, is a knot of silent ones surrounded by picture books. One of them comes up to greet me and leads me off. A far cry indeed from my own full-time teaching past or from any centre of secondary education I know of. There's no mistaking a good primary school. I was smitten with the passionate thought that this child dragging me along would be wise to make the most of the now, before shades of the secondary prison house begin to close around her — but I was through the door of the classroom that was expecting me before I had time to examine such a notion rationally. A very different classroom, so very new to me. A primary classroom. Suddenly, I longed for my own professional four walls.

These days, when I see teachers hunched under impossible administrative loads and bombarded by the sneers of officialdom and the gutter press, I am glad to be out of the profession. Even so, I miss my own classroom. There are compensations in staying put on the job. There, all endeavours may be geared to the specific nature and needs of the children one has come to know. There is a security in such knowing. I find nowadays, as a rootless traveller through other people's classrooms, I am caught in a dilemma: it's now or never; I've got to do it right first time; for me there are no tomorrows with which to make a new start. Yet I know very well that the best of doing emerges from seeing beyond the immediacies of the moment (which, in this case, I bring) and behind the faces on view. I can never throw off anxiety caused by my own total ignorance of the individual identities of the strangers gazing at me, the stranger. At best I am allowed mere tasters of this huge resource. At best, therefore, everything depends on the quality of the classroom ethos that has already been established and, more so, upon the follow-up work after I have closed the door behind me. I have become better able to address that realisation as such visits have multiplied.

So — there I was, inside a classroom again, but not mine. Having played Gulliver to Rosalind's Lilliputians, now I found myself among 10-year-olds at the request of their teacher, Pat, my one-time next-door neighbour. Again a sea of unfamiliar faces ... but it was good to know their teacher well. Our first eye contact that day was redolent of shared laughter, shared glooms, stories too numerous to recollect and a mutual confidence in the shared present. Unlike all future occasions, I entered that classroom as myself, recognisable to me because of being so to my friend. Among our thousand topics of chat and chinwag, we had talked teaching many times. We knew our wavelength. There and then we established without a word that we were collaborators, for the afternoon and beyond, in fostering productive linguistic and social experience within her classroom.

This is quite different from appearing on the scene like a conjurer or his white rabbit. Enter stage left the professional entertainer, the creator of diversions, the breaker of routines, the Visiting Performer. Oh no, that's not for me! Neither, therefore, will there be any genuflection from the incumbent adult, nor its converse — a red pen poised over a pile of exercise books in a convenient back corner — thank you very much!

The performer works like magic so expectations of him are high indeed, but I am a teacher and cannot work magic — though a story told will be much more likely to do so than any other form of discourse. The performer, it seems, has all the fun (and a fee) with no responsibility for the past or the future of his young audience. He will consider any pupils' misdemeanours to be none of his business yet will feel free to object to any class teacher who slips anxiously into the wardress role. This makes everybody nervous, including me when I am perceived as a performer. I want to say — don't worry about these bairns, I know how you feel, I am a teacher too, we could swop places if you learned to care about story-telling. There are, too, those times when I am aware of a certain resentment because I am not a real full-time worker ... worker? How does work come in when it all seems to be so easy, relaxed and benign? Then I want to shout — I've done my stint in the salt mines, you know! And it takes a lot of preparation to tell a story as if the whole thing is flowing out spontaneously: I've done my homework, you know!

Of course I don't say these things. I have found my own means of delivering the message that I enter the classroom as a co-worker. Whatever else, at least there is always the comfort of my faith in the power of a good tale to take over all spirits, even anxious or ruffled ones, just as my story did in Pat's classroom that day where there was no need at all for me to explain myself.

In no time the children were circled around in a close group, the front half seated on the carpeted floor, the rest on chairs or tables close behind. For my own self-confidence and without any questioning of its suitability for the age group, I had chosen to tell my favourite story, guaranteed to hold any group, *The Land Where No One Ever Dies* (Part 3, page 132). Soon I had plucked the child of this particular once-upon-a-time out of his peaceful, uneventful village world and set him on his impossible quest for a place where there is no death. In his journeying he rejects three offers, of one, two then three hundred years' worth of longevity and eventually arrives at a castle on a mountain top where the oldest man imaginable assures him that he has all Time ahead of him. *"Come in," says the old man, "I have long waited for you and I shall be glad of your company." And so time passes in the castle where no one ever dies.*

But the moment comes when the boy is smitten with longing to see his family and friends again, just once. He sets off on the return journey on horseback, with the old man's warning ringing in his ears: *"Do not dismount, for if you do, you will be as other mortals are, and Death will take you!"* He travels across a landscape strangely changed from that which he had crossed before and, likewise, the village of his birth is hardly recognisable, with its stone cottages transformed to houses of brick. When the truth dawns upon him that all that was once familiar has passed away long since, he spurs his horse to full speed towards the castle and its eternal security. Of course he does not reach it. On the winding track up the mountain, as dusk falls fast, he encounters an old fellow who is trying vainly to pull his hand cart out of a muddy ditch, a cart piled high with worn-out boots and shoes. And of course the boy is persuaded to step down upon the ground to give his aid.

And so I reached the climax of a story which must have taken getting on for three quarters of an hour to tell to this motionless group of children.

"Got you at last!" I cry, grabbing Pat's right arm. Involuntarily — and conveniently for me — she gives a shriek. *"Look at the boots and shoes I have worn out in my search for you over the wide world! I am Death, and no one escapes my clutch!"* With that, all the centuries that had passed came upon the boy. He wrinkled, crumpled and shrank, smaller, smaller until he disappeared into the damp earth.

I gaze into the faces before me. What an impact, I tell myself, what a story! Except that one face before me is registering total horror. Something must be done and quickly.

We were all enveloped in the finality of that silence which always follows a successful tale-telling. I had no ending in my repertoire other than the one I had spoken so what could have been the source of the words that insinuated themselves into that silence?

That, you might think, is the end of the story, I hear myself confiding. But the end of the story was not to be seen for it was within the boy's own mind. Let me tell you what he saw in his head the very instant that the old man grasped his arm. There before him, as if in a framed picture, appeared the grey stone front of the cottage where he had been born, where he had lived in such contentment until his restless travels began. And there, in the open doorway, stood his mother, smiling at him, her hair and skin shining in what seemed to him to be morning sunlight. She lifted her arms towards him. "Come in," she said, "I have long waited for you and I shall be glad of your company." The boy smiled back and stepped over the frame, into the picture.

This ending visibly relaxed the little girl for whom it was intended. I am not suggesting that it is a remarkable piece of invention — it is no better and no worse than the many alternative endings I have heard offered since that afternoon, in workshops and classrooms where I have told the same story and asked for changes to the story. What is significant, however, is that the process of its emergence was quite different from any off-the-cuff adaptations to the needs of my audience that I had made in the past.

Let me explain what I mean. At certain moments in storytelling one might be aware that a word, phrase or idea has struck a wrong note or held up the meaning. One can quickly reword, rephrase and so re-establish intent without impeding the flow. Such repetitions rarely come amiss in oral storytelling. At other times there may be some interruption, perhaps a genuinely spontaneous outburst from a listener, or laughter which drifts into a little battery of comments or, from time to time, a less welcome disruptive intrusion — someone's foot pokes the back of the person in front or a child comes into the room to collect her belongings or the school bell sounds. This kind of thing I have learned to cope with, quite often incorporating some reference to the unexpected event as a relevant parenthesis to the story. Such moments can throw a first-time storyteller right off her stroke but it is surprising how quickly one learns to cope with them as confidence in storytelling takes over. If I cannot incorporate the interruption (another teacher comes into the room, for instance, and takes time about his business before going off) I simply wait with my mouth shut and let a silence descend and remain until I know everyone's eager for the next bit of the story. I should add that perhaps, in a very general kind of way there is always adaptation to the overall mood or character of an audience; one gets the 'feel' of the group and finds oneself shifting somewhat in style and tone to fit into the setting.

But the 'interruption' which took the form of a child's distress at the end of my story that afternoon initiated a major change in the content of the story (and therefore its impact and import) which was of a totally different order in my experience up to that point. This particular product of the immediate circumstances drew upon an area of my imagination which up to then I had associated exclusively with the preparatory work before, not during, a storytelling.

I still believe that there are people whose imaginations are much more powerful than the norm — itself pretty powerful! — which bubble and ferment insatiably once underway. These are the 'naturals' among storytellers; we hear them on the media and read them in literature and sometimes encounter them among our friends on social occasions. My story here is about you and me. My imagination has to do some hard graft to get a story ready for telling. The major part of my preparation for a storytelling is to build up, bit by bit, a clear visual image of each major shift in the action of the story: slow work. What my tongue in the event describes is a procession of those images as described in Chapter 5 of *And None of it was Nonsense*. They are crucial and immutable. Any commentary or reflection upon them evolves without a need for rehearsal as such, as does most of the dialogue between participants in the story. If these visual props are fully realised beforehand the spoken words seem to flow naturally out of them. Without these mental pictures there would be no integrity or apparent effortlessness in the delivery of the tale, so I am careful to fix them in my head before I start. This time, however, one such image had popped into my mind spontaneously, instantly and complete. As a bonus, the mother spoke in words which reflected those of the old man in the castle when he first greeted the boy, complementing (I felt) the significance of this new image.

My conclusion is that involvement in the flow of a told story engenders creativity. I had, after all, delighted in the evidence of this a hundred times from my own ex-pupils' re-tellings of my stories but this was the first time I was conscious of the same thing happening spontaneously to me while telling a story. It really took me by surprise. Clearly, the more practice one has in storytelling, the more nimble the imagination becomes and the further one moves from those early attempts to 'learn' someone else's story. Thus one's confidence is boosted as a storyteller.

An obvious corollary to all this is that the storyteller has total freedom to modify a story at any time, perhaps in response to the dictates of an active imagination within or in adapting to the moment-by-moment effect of the story upon the audience without, or both simultaneously. While such changes exemplify the process of making a story one's own, they also underline the interactive nature of an experience shared by teller and listeners.

Each new occasion contains a stimulating challenge. A good storytelling is never quite the same twice.

Chapter 5
IS MY TALE TOO FRIGHTENING?

On my way home from Pat's classroom I found myself pondering the appropriateness of the story for that age-group. In principle, a good story is a good story, irrespective of the age of the recipients. Traditionally, folk stories accommodate people of all ages simultaneously and this particular tale was a splendid example of one which needed no modifications to take hold of young and old alike. However, I had incorporated into the telling, at an early stage in the story, the death of the boy's much-loved grandmother: how could I know what bereavement-trauma might be stored up in the memory of some child in my audience and painfully activated by my words? More than this was the fact that the inevitability of death (strangely sombre food for thought inside heads which are closer to their birth than their demise) underpinned the entire plot.

My storyteller's instinct rebelled against making changes of the sort I had indulged in on that occasion and even more so against excluding it from the primary classroom. *The Land Where No One Ever Dies* appealed enormously to me, which is the essential prerequisite for telling a story well; and equally, perhaps for similar reasons, it worked supremely well for the pupils themselves who had been entranced into silent stillness during the entire telling. The impromptu syrup I had concocted at the finish had perhaps robbed the tale of its authenticity. I had lightened to the point of altering completely the basic burden of the tale by sugaring the ending. And endings are important. Listening to a story one is aware of a pleasing and perpetual state of enjoying the moment for itself, while at the same time reaching out for the final resolution: a nice dichotomy. If the actual conclusion fails to fit, the story itself in retrospect becomes a waste of time, even an unwelcome disturbance — as the 'original' ending proved to be for one member of the audience that afternoon.

Certainly the 'true' folk ending is ferocious. It startles, however momentarily, not in a Hammer film horror or blunderbuss kind of way, but insidiously, prodding at one's equilibrium. Here, fair is foul and foul is fair. Death is a devious sneak. He moves in for the kill only after his old bones have evoked pity. Fee fi fo fum from a giant and fire on a dragon's breath is healthy stuff indeed compared with the smile on the face of the tiger, or the wheedling tones of a wicked queen over Snow White's poisoned apple, or the sight of a house made of sweets which contains an evil witch bent on the destruction of Hansel and Gretel. Better the devil you know any time! If there has to be an iron hand, let it not affect a velvet glove.

Old and young are prepared to return to such symbols in the world of make-believe over and over again. We do not reject them, whether it's "Read it again, Mummy" for another viewing of Aladdin's uncle, or one's umpteenth encounter with Macbeth — the deceived deceiver — later on in life. Perhaps in the final answer we need metaphorical representation of life's surprise attacks. Most catastrophes come unannounced in the midst of innocuous normality and even when the worst is anticipated, the actual event still shocks. My story had spoken these things and that was its strength. And yet, and yet ... how early in life is such symbolism cathartic? And at what age is it acceptable to receive a tale which gives catastrophe the last word?

Even the very young are subject to life's darker side. There is a place for narrative/poetic representation of fearful things just as soon as things appear fearful. So it is that children enjoy such books as *Where the Wild Things Are* and *Can't you Sleep, Little Bear?* I have no doubt that the more a child is entertained by tales of surmountable fearful fantasies, the less that child is oppressed by the phantoms which threaten from within his or her own personal darkness. Indeed, as every parent knows, a nightlight or, if the worst comes to the worst, the comforting presence of a trusted parent, is a far more effective antidote to midnight monsters than any sensible assurance of a "But there's nothing there, dear, now go to sleep" type. While rational explanation is always preferable to a pack of lies, however young the child, it doesn't necessarily convince. A good tale, on the other hand, which carries the message that ghoulies and ghosties and long-leggedy beasties can be rendered harmless, is likely to touch a much more receptive area of a young child's consciousness.

More disturbing than fear of the dark must be fear of the tangible. It is a sad fact of our times that most violence emanates among people who see each other everyday rather than from the stranger; and most violence is perpetrated against the most vulnerable — women, children and small children especially, whose lives are sometimes anything but cosy. If school is to have any significance in the totality of children's experience I do not think it should always speak with a hushed, honeyed tongue. I always feel a prickle of suspicion when I enter an infant classroom where every word is sweet.

I am not suggesting for one moment, though, that teachers should provide children with representations of a nasty world because the world is a something of a nasty place — this is as destructive as the argument that pupils must vie with each other in the classroom rather than cooperate in order to prepare them for a competitive world! In general the opposite is the case: a powerful solace in misery is absorption in some intriguing occupation. A school which offers a plethora of attractive activities can prove an oasis for troubled youngsters. It might even generate in the process the kind of self-confidence necessary for coping more effectively with the world outside. But the source of real fear will not go away for some, especially those who cannot find words to describe it or ears to hear. Even the first classroom of all must provide a climate where the child feels there is space for the 'nasties' he or she may need to bring through the school gates.

The symbolic representation of fearsome things through the safe medium of folk story may well help the intent listener to come to terms with real-life pain. At the very least, suffering within a story may serve to relieve the loneliness, the sense of isolation, which hedge about the real-life sufferer who hears it. Sometimes, too, empathetic tears from a member of the audience at a storytelling are not necessarily a bad thing. In the absence of palpable companions in sorrow, perhaps fictitious ones will do, for a while, at least. It seems to me that a folk story can move the listener to a compassion which may be directed inwards, in the case of those who suffer or have suffered, as well as outwards for the many. This is a salutary thing, like mourning. The same can apply where there is empathy with narrative characters who experience some natural loss — like the death of a granny. Tears can soothe and heal.

Not everyone will agree. To some extent my argument is suspect in so far as I am susceptible to children's tears and will do anything to skirt round a likely encounter. But I cannot avoid the knowledge that individuals who have been thus moved by the sorrowful events of some stories I tell have quite clearly been appreciative of the experience. This has been in evidence on several occasions during adult workshops with primary and secondary teachers and once at a conference for English advisers, when participants in small group discussion have chosen to talk precisely and openly about events which have given rise to their feelings. On all but one occasion the particular pain which had caused the tears was something that had occurred during childhood but not put into words at the time. If individuals find comfort in being thus profoundly moved, is it right to deprive children of the sensation? As Bruno Bettelheim puts it in *The Uses of Enchantment*:

Many parents believe that only conscious reality or pleasant and wish-fulfilling images should be presented to the child — that he should be exposed only to the sunny side of things. But such one-sided fare nourishes the mind only in a one-sided way ...

Modern stories written for young children mainly avoid ... existential problems, although they are crucial issues for all of us. The child needs most particularly to be given suggestions in symbolic form about how he may deal with these issues and grow safely into maturity. 'Safe' stories mention neither death nor aging, the limits to our existence, nor the wish for eternal life. The fairy tale, by contrast, confronts the child squarely with the basic human predicaments.

My own experience of storytelling leads me to accept the basic premise of Bettelheim's absorbing writing — that is, that children should not be subjected to lobotomised versions of folk/fairy tales — though I find his detailed Freudian interpretations of individual stories less easy to swallow. A more 'child-centred' account (though less readable — distinctively the off-shoot of a doctorate thesis) of a young reader's interpretation of a folk tale, put forward in the light of the difficulties and upsets within the child's own world, is given by Jeff Adams in *The Conspiracy of the Text*. On the frightening aspects of stories he has this to say:

It is not a case of children reading 'because they like to be frightened' but rather in order to find out about important problems they are faced with as they grow up; cultural artefacts lodge the answers in insecurity.

I believe very strongly that as teachers our main sin is to underestimate the perceptions of children. They can respond to more than we allow them. Reactions which an English adviser (or, perhaps I should say, an adult) is glad to describe with sensitivity may be very close to those of a young child. But the child will not have either the vocabulary or the sense of audience required for articulating a justification for his or her own reception of a sombre tale. Very young children are, in my experience, capable of quite subtle and serious reflection.

I suppose as a storyteller one has to use one's instinct in deciding what is too this or that for a particular audience. What would one choose, for instance, to entertain a group of bedridden children in a hospice for the terminally ill? I hope I will never have to face such decision-making but I know of an American storyteller who did and I have a written version of the choice she made, a story she has told in such a situation several times over — so it must have been right. It was brought to my attention by Heather Sharpe, a storyteller from Leeds. The voice and location of *Mr Death and the Red Headed Woman* is obvious with the first words:

Mr Death came riding over the plains on his pale stallion. He came riding right into town, down mainstreet, past the Wells Fargo Office and when he got to the Bluebird Saloon ...

It is a truly wonderful story, full of lyricism, humour — and energy engendered largely by the resourceful heroine of the tale, the red-headed Maude Applegate, who pursues Mr Death and travels around the world with him twice, in order to save the life of Billy Bantree, her (no-good, womanisin', whisky-drinkin', card-playin') sweetheart. In spite of his trade, at home with his granny Mr Death turns out to be a very merry fellow indeed, partial to a glass of home-made blackberry wine, a good sing-song and the playing of jigs on his fiddle. While practising his profession, he proves to be wise, loving and caring: this version heavily emphasises the service he performs, and the gentleness of it. He is, of course, lonely, so it is a great relief when Maude Applegate finally sees the light, gets her priorities right and teams up with Death: ... *and they say to this day she takes a real interest in her husband's work and in her own right she adopts another role, which is that of one who soothingly sings little children to sleep when they retire for the night.*

I have told this story to school children with enormous success and once, at the London Narrative Group, to adults. One member of the group, Tony Addison, must have wrapped it up warm to take home: he told a friend the story and, many weeks later, I received what she wrote as a result. I was very excited to read Judith Baresel's unsolicited creation (see Part 3, page 137).

If I found myself in the unimaginable position of telling a story to a dying child I doubt if I would have the courage to tell a story about death, real or personified. And yet there must inevitably be risk-taking in storytelling, as in teaching. Who is to know what apparently innocuous reference one can make which causes offence or hurt? A young teacher might well incorporate an 'in' obscenity without realising it, or unwittingly make a remark unseemly to a Muslim or Hindu; how easy for a maths teacher to refer to the 'the final solution', little realising the significance of the expression in the head of a Jewish listener.

During a coffee break at that English advisers' conference workshop we were talking about the importance of disseminating information concerning pupils' personal difficulties among their teachers. Someone described an occasion when he learned quite by chance just before a sixth form lesson that the father of one of the students he was about to teach had committed suicide the night before by putting his head in the gas oven. It was thought better for her to go to school as usual, apparently. The teacher had intended to discuss with the students Wilfred Owen's poem *Dulce et Decorum est*, with its grisly account of a soldier stricken by gas in the First World War. I need hardly say he changed his plans, fast.

Certainly if instinct tells that a story will offer balm and welcome insight, then there is a place for it. However, when it comes to the pre-school child at bedtime or in the nursery, it is perhaps as well to be especially wary over what might touch a raw nerve. From time to time in choosing a story I will seek to inspire reflection within a young audience without rubbing their noses in gloom and doom.

I think I was right on that occasion in Pat's classroom to sweeten the pill at the end of *The Land Where No one Ever Dies* for the sake of one person. But I have no regrets over telling the story to 9- and 10-year-olds and have done so several times since. I don't think I would tell it to children very much younger. I would tell stories in any classroom which involve real fears and sorrows, being very careful about the relevance of the events to the lives of the children, and the resolution of those events: like Bettelheim, I believe that narratives should offer hope rather than despair.

Several months after my visit to Pat's pupils she told me that they still made reference to the story I had told, sometimes at the most unlikely moments. One day in a classroom which was unfailingly hospitable to animal guests, as well as human, from tiddler to tortoise, she was unexpectedly confronted by her one phobia — a snake. This called forth an unteacherly scream, "Just like when Death grabbed you by the arm, miss!" remarked the snake's owner.

Before I left her room at the end of my visit, Pat told me more about the children. There was Terry who was highly disturbed, put in that class until a place was found for him in a special educational unit, because of the teacher's exceptional capacity to cope with 'difficult' children. He was the one she was worried about and who had given her some reservations about inviting me. She said she had never seen him sit so still, listening, for so long. There was Roger who was Polish. He had begun learning English when he came to this country eighteen months previously. He had apparently followed the story and in fact he came to talk to me about it afterwards.

This was to be the first of many occasions when early stage bilingual learners and pupils with behavioural problems were to respond far more favourably to hearing a story than to any other classroom activity. At times, such responses are acknowledged by the teachers with a joy bordering on incredulity. On every occasion — without exception — that I have told a story in someone's classroom I am told of this child or that who has never before sat so still, listening; and on every occasion — again, without exception — in written follow-up work, there will be pupils excelling themselves in quantity and in quality where they would normally produce nothing or a reluctant little.

A particularly pleasant occasion for me was when I told this same story to a class of 10-year-olds, having been informed moments before I began that the little girl sitting just under my nose was severely deaf. There were a lot of phrases and sentences repeated with different wording in that particular rendering and at times I must have sounded like someone in the throes of an elocution lesson! That evening, so I was told, the child delighted her mother with her version of the story and the next day she re-told it into a tape recorder (as did most of the other children in the group) in the presence of her special needs teacher, who saw her effort as a major step forward. Several children in that class had experienced, some months previously, the death of a classmate from leukaemia. Had I known I would probably have chosen a different story; had her teacher known what I was going to tell, she would probably have warned me against it. We would both have been wrong. They were able to refer more comfortably to that, and other deaths they had known, after listening to the story, according to their teacher.

I have many utterly delightful new versions of this story, both spoken and written, from 10-year-old children, produced during follow-up lessons after my visits. I will conclude with an extract from a tape recording made by one of them.

... as he was riding he saw this little old man wheeling this big barrow of shoes and boots all with holes in, and he thought, I wonder if he is coming to try to sell them to us. If he is, he can get ... he can go away. I don't want to buy no shoes with holes in. And there was this poor little donkey leading it up and he was hitting it with a whip and Paul felt very sad for the poor donkey. So the old man called out, then he, the old man called out, "Hello, young man' (she adopts a rasping, faltering voice) *"I'm trying to get this up here but I can't. Will you help me?" Paul remembered he wasn't allowed off the horse so he said, "But I can't get off my horse. I'm sorry, old fellow." And so the man goes, "Oh, go on!" So Paul thought, if I just step off for a few minutes, could I...? Oh, I'm going to get off. And then he — got — off — the horse* (slow, tragic tones followed next by a big speed-up) *one foot on the ground and the man grabbed hold of him, going, "I am Death* (spat out, furiously) *I have been looking for you everywhere. These are the boots and shoes I have worn out looking for you. Now I have got you." And he strangled Paul! And he dropped dead! And then the old man* (in the castle) *looked out of his window and he was a wizard really and he put this flash of lightning on the old man and he DIED!*

Caroline, the teller here, had produced a very long, complex and ingeniously original version which she told to a tape recorder with considerable dramatic sense and many 'voices'. Later on she did a different written version, minuscule by comparison: her teacher said, "Now *there's* a storyteller! — but she can't write." Well, we teachers know what she means. It comes as a surprise to encounter a really reluctant writer among our pupils who is otherwise outgoing and creatively articulate. The following was the result of a special effort on Caroline's part.

Once upon a time there was a boy called paul and he didn't want to dye so he said to his mum and dad on day "i dont want to dye" "but you have to dye one day" his parents said "we all have to dye some day" so the boy went out to serch for the place where you never dye so the boy walked for days on end and one day he came to a lady with short brown hair and he said "do you know where the land of never dye is " and she said "if you can stay with me because i have to dig a hole 100 miles deep and then you will dye" "how long will that take you" said paul "about 100 years" the lady said "but i want to live for ever" well you can't live forever round here" so the boy went on his way after another day walking he came to another lady with hair that came down to her waist and the boy said "is this the land where you live for ever" "now" said the lady "but i have to sell all these shoes and boots but kno one ever comes past only about 20 people a year so it will take me about 200 years then i will dye" "but i want to live forever said the boy well you will have to be on your way then because you will never live for ever hear" so the boy went on his way and after about another day he came to a lady that was very tall with brown hair down to her feet and the boy said "is this the land where you live forever" and the girl said "you can live for ever here as long as you put these shoes on Ive been trying to sell them for 100 years thank you can i come to live with you because i have not got a family because they have all dyed so paul put the shoes on and they went back to his own land and they were married and lived happily ever after.

There is material for a short book simply in Caroline's two versions of this story, especially if placed in the context of her classroom where there was a rich storytelling environment created by an unusually gifted teacher. Anyone who reads her first draft quoted here and the short extract from her oral version above it will find plenty of food for thought and discussion. Suffice it for me to make two observations only. First, a 10-year-old will respond remarkably creatively to hearing *The Land Where No One Ever Dies*. Secondly, children (even very young ones indeed, as I shall show later) will find their own 'satisfactory' resolutions to stories and should be encouraged to do so. In Caroline's case, she deals out due retribution to sneaky old Death in her oral retelling while her less relaxed mode — the written form — leads her to the conventional 'happy ever after' ending of folk/romance fiction.

As my Aberdeenshire mother-in-law used to say, "We a' have our ain way."

And a good thing too.

Chapter 6
FIVE-YEAR OLDS AND *THE GIANT OVER THE MOUNTAIN*

I have been into many primary schools since, and been back to Rosalind's nursery several times with tales of thieving monkeys from somewhere in Africa, of a singing drum from Somalia, of mice hidden in Douglas fircones from North America to name but a few.

One thing's for sure: it's more peaceful telling stories in the nursery than telling *The Giant over the Mountain* to seventy 4/5-year-olds accompanied by the birdsong — chirrups and squawks predominating — of three free-flying budgies! I meant to ask the headteacher if the birds were at all housetrained. The children were, at least as far as the raucous birdnoise was concerned: it was only when I had almost finished that it dawned on me that these infants were so used to their winged companions that they barely registered their presence. On the other hand, I had to suffer the urge, heavy upon me throughout, to wring their little green necks.

This is how it was. The occasion is as faithfully transcribed as the budgie-bugged tape allows.

Teacher: Her name is Betty. Show Betty how nicely you sit. Thank you, Sam. Thank you Matthew.

Mutter mutter.

Well. You ready?

Chirrup.

Teacher: Matthew. Matthew.

I'm going to tell you a story today

Yeeeeeh.

A story about being afraid. Know what I mean?

Being afraid of the dark.

When I was little sometimes I was afraid of the dark but there wasn't really anything there, but I didn't know that and I thought there was. There's a friend that I have who told me that when she was a little girl the thing she was really afraid of was going to the dentist, you know, and her mother used to tell her a story before she went to the dentist and it's the story I'm going to tell you in a minute. Now is there somebody here who can tell me about something you're afraid of? Oh yes, there are lots ... What are you afraid of?

I'm afraid of the wolf.
I'm afraid of the ghosts.
I'm scared of ghosts.
Monsters.
D'you know summing ...?
The wolf! The wolf!
D'you know summing, when I went on holiday one night I saw a wolf and I wasn't scared of it.

You weren't scared of it?

The dark.
I'm scared of the dark ... (Mutter-mutter, noisier than before ...)

Right. You're just the people for me to tell my story to.

What about him?

I'm going to save him up. And you. You can tell me your stories afterwards, OK?

This is the story my friend's mum used to tell her when she was going to go to the dentist. She didn't have to be afraid of the dentist because dentists are all right really but she thought the dentist was a bit like the big bad wolf. Or a giant. Or a monster.

Or a ghost.

Or a ghost. And she got so afraid before she went. And that was the worst part — before she went. She'd think oh! Oh! It's terrible — but when she actually got into the dentist's chair it was always fine! Well, this is the story that my friend's mum used to tell her beforehand.

Ready?

Chirrup chirrup.

Once upon a time there was a little village where everybody was very happy.

Chirrup chirrup.

And they had lots of birds about and they liked that and they had lots of things to eat in their garden and there was lots of fish in the sea that the fishermen would catch, you see, so everybody was very pleased with it all. Now there was one thing that they were afraid of, and shall I tell you what it was?

Yeees!

They were afraid ...

The dentist?

... Not the dentist, no, they didn't mind that. They were afraid of a giant who everybody said lived on the other side of the mountain, on the other side of the mountain — the village was by the mountain there and the sea was over there and all the people in the village whispered to each other ... "Don't go over the mountain. Don't go over the mountain because of the giant man who will eat you all up." So they were full of fear of the giant who lived on the other side of the mountain. And they knew he lived there even though they hadn't seen him because their mums and dads had told them about him. And when their mums and dads were little, their mums and dads had told them about it and the grandads and grandmas, and the great-grand parents and the great-great-grand parents, all the people for a long, long time all said to each other ... "Don't go up the mountain because on the other side of the mountain is the giant!"

Chirrup chirrup squawk.

Even while the birds are chirrupping and singing, on the other side of the mountain is the huge giant.

There was one little girl in the village and she was living in that village with her mum and dad. Her mum and dad had come to live there about twenty years before my story happened. Now all the other children in the village — their parents and their grand parents and their great-grand parents, oh, for as long as you can think of, had lived in that village. But not this little girl's family. Her name was Dawn and her mum and dad had come from Jamaica which is in the West Indies, and they'd come over to the village because they wanted to find a new place to live. And this little girl heard them whispering to each other one day, she heard them saying, "Don't go over the mountain.

Don't go over the mountain because there is a giant over the mountain."
Well, Dawn began to ask people about the giant, What was he like? Did he
have long claws? Did he have big long fangs? Did he have big poppy eyes?
Did he have a nasty frown over his head? Did he roar ahrrrrr? But nobody
could tell her, because nobody had seen the giant over the mountain, because
nobody had been up the mountain. They just knew there was a giant over
there but they'd never seen him and they didn't know what he looked like.
Well, Dawn was a very brave girl, you know, and she decided she was going
to go up the mountain. She wanted to see ... she wanted to see the giant so
she decided, when nobody was looking she'd climb up the mountain and see
the giant for herself.

So she decided she'd go in the middle of the night because then nobody would
try to stop her if she went in the middle of the night. So she went to bed as
usual and she waited until it was very dark. The moon came up and the moon
was full and it shone down on all the houses and on all the birds and the birds'
wings when they were still and everything shone silver in the moonlight. And
she could see how she could get up the mountain on her own because it was lit
up by the moon.

She came downstairs when everybody was in bed asleep, and tiptoed into the
kitchen. She got some cheese and some bread and she went out of the back door
with her little bag on her back with her bread and cheese in. By the light of the
moon she started to climb the mountain. She climbed and climbed (chirrup
chirrup) and the birds were startled by what she was doing and some of them
fluttered about and squealed like that. But nobody else moved. Everybody was
asleep in their beds.

Can you remember what was on the other side of the mountain?

Giant!
The giant.

And she was a bit afraid when she thought ... but she was a brave girl and she
said, "I'm not going to be afraid! I'm not going to be afraid! I'm going to see
the giant."

And by the time she was half way up the mountain the sun was coming up
over the sea. It was lighting up all the houses and the people were beginning to
wake up, and Dawn's mother woke up and she was saying, "Where is she?
Where is my baby? Where is my little girl?" She wasn't in her bed. She
wasn't hiding anywhere. It was time for school. Dawn, who was now three-
quarters of the way up the mountain, nearly at the top of the mountain, from

where she was she could hear the sound of the school bell and the little high pitched cries of children who were going to school. And her mother was saying, "Where's Dawn? I can't find her!" And she knocked on her neighbours' doors and she told her neighbours, "I've lost Dawn. I don't know where she is. Will you help me look for her?" And all the neighbours came to look for Dawn ...

She's over the mountain.

But you see ... she was, but nobody thought to look up the mountain because nobody ever climbed up the mountain — because they knew that on the other side of the mountain was ...

A giant, there was a giant!

... Aaahhh! But Dawn was just having a little bite of cheese and a bit of bread from out of her bag that she'd taken up. She was nearly ready to climb over the top and look — and she thought she'd better have a full tummy, whatever was on the other side she'd better have something to eat. She put the paper back into her bag and she did up the zip and she put it over her shoulder again and she climbed the last little bit to the top of the mountain. And she looked over the top and there, right at the bottom of the mountain in the dark shadow — because the sun hadn't come up high enough to light it up — in the dark shadow at the bottom there was a great big figure, sitting with his back to her, a great big thing with a great big head and huge shoulders.

For a moment Dawn was very frightened because she knew that was the giant!

And then, he had sharp claws.

Do you know she couldn't see whether he had sharp claws or not because his hands were tucked like this. She could only see the shape of him — his great big head and his great big shoulders sitting there and she thought to herself, "I wonder if he has got sharp claws" and she thought, "I wonder what he looks like" and she forgot to be afraid because she wanted to know what he looked like, you know? So she started to slither her way down the mountain towards the great big giant. And do you know, when she was climbing down the mountain a very very surprising thing happened. You won't believe this it's so amazing. As she got nearer to the giant, instead of getting bigger as things do when you get nearer to them — like I'm bigger now, aren't I?

No (from Matthew).

... than when I'm down over here. Instead of the giant getting bigger, he got smaller! She looked at him and she thought, "That's very strange." She went further on and he got smaller and smaller so that when she got right up to the giant, do you know, he came only up to her ankle? And she stood there and she looked at this tiny little man and she said, "But you're only a little man!" And she picked him up off the ground in her cupped hands. And she looked at him and said, "You're not a giant! You're just a little man!" And the little man looked up at her, and said, "I'm not a giant. My name is Fear."

(Sniffs. silence. Staring. Waiting for the rest???)

Now isn't that amazing? And when she told the people in the village — 'cause she went back over the mountain and went back to the village, and was her mum pleased to see her I can tell you! ...

Was he a nice monster?

He was lovely! He was only a little tiny man like that.

Didn't he want to grow bigger? Was he magic and he growed right to the bottom?

Well, I think it was a kind of magic. But you know I think that sometimes the people said to themselves, well, fancy being afraid like that. It was just our own fear that made us think it was a big giant. We thought he was a big giant but he wasn't a big giant — just a little fellow.

Did she take the giant back with her?

Sure. He rode in her bag with the bits of wrapping paper from the cheese. They all liked him a lot ... Now is there any clever person here ...?

Me (from Matthew).

... Who ... you are? Well, one of you, could you tell me why my friend's mum used to tell her that story before she took her to the dentist?

Because she was frightened ... or not

Well, yes ... er, 'or not' she didn't have to be frightened. Can someone else tell me?

Because, because they think the giant is a giant and he isn't. And because the mum told her that it isn't a giant before she visited the dentist so she'd remember that it wasn't a giant, the dentist wasn't a giant.

You are so right. And what did you want to tell me?

Well, they thought he was there but there wasn't a giant there all the time.

I'm not afraid of monsters!

You're not? Neither am I.

I'm not afraid neither.
Nor me.
I'm not.
I've got one. I've got one ...

Come on then, tell me.

... I'm not afraid either.

There followed a general chorus/discussion/mutual assurance, with budgie accompaniment, to the effect that no one was afraid of monsters or giants or ghosts ... At least, it was clearly no longer *de rigueur* to show anything that was less than total bravado. How very accommodating infants can be. In fact from my experiences at the nursery and visits such as this one I have decided that infants are very loveable little creeps! Here, to start with they wanted to tell me (who had come to tell them a story about fear) how they are afraid of EVERYTHING. At the finish (when I had proved that fear is vincible) they wanted to tell me how they are afraid of NOTHING. Being a Betty rather than a Bettelheim I am not sure how much of the 'message' actually stuck!

What is interesting is that this story suits the taste of any age-group from 4 to adulthood — give or take a little bit at its denouement. I hadn't been too sure how I would cope with the ending, hence the preamble about dentists, so I was prepared for any necessary adaptation according to the response of the audience. Clearly the punch line, "My name is Fear" would not have much clout with little ones though it's fine for older children and adults. Fortunately I was able to rely on the fact that the younger child is more open in responding to a story so it was easy for me to pick up their subsequent demands and doubts: Dawn finishes up happily reunited with her mum and the locals, while the 'giant' is readily available to add to the merriment in the village of each child's imagination.

Chapter 7
A WELSH GIANT FOR ADOLESCENTS AND ADULTS

I have since used the story of *The Giant over the Mountain* in its simplest form with even younger children and, with some secondary classes and adults, in a much more elaborate version. Let me say a word about the former because it throws yet more light on the question of what is right for which age-group and how a storyteller must adjust.

It was an occasion at Rosalind's nursery when a story was demanded of me off the cuff. I really wasn't in the mood and had a kind of blank — me, tell a story? I don't know any. I'm not ready ... I launched myself into *The Giant over the Mountain* without the necessary silent pre-contemplation. I told it without any of the identity kits of the folk involved or silver moonlight on the midnight tiles or birdsong or school bell to ring in the ears of the heroine. What was there in good measure, however, were the intense whispers ... *"Don't go over the mountain. Don't go over the mountain because the giant is there."* I should have detected the anxious looks long before I did. When the girl began her trek up the mountainside suddenly one of the toddlers leapt into Rosalind's arms with a horrible wailing, "No! No! Not up the mountain, Rosalind!"

End of event. The best retrieval I could muster was to heartily assure everybody present that it was all perfectly all right really because when she got there she found that there wasn't a giant at all, only a tiny little man who was lovely really and all the villagers were very pleased with him when she took him back to show her mum.

Not exactly what you'd call storytelling. Not exactly the most perceptive of storytellers. Someday I'll try it again, though, because I am quite sure the fault was in the telling not in the tale: tone of voice and body language can determine the level of fearsomeness of a fearful tale better than the actual words of an oral story.

I took my more elaborate version of this story to a class of 14/15-year-olds in a multi-ethnic secondary school. It's possible to do what I did at the outset, which was to tell most of the story in one sentence:

Once there was a village where the people were very content but for the fact that on the other side of the mountain which towered over the village they knew there was a giant, feared by everyone except for one brave little girl who, all by herself one moonlit night, climbed up to the top of the slope and down the other side, to see the giant for herself and on her way down, an extraordinary thing happened before her very eyes ...

You all want to know what happened, don't you?

And, of course, such is the power of story that they all patently did.

I'll tell you what happened but I'll begin at the beginning.

There was once a village. To the north and south of it stretched a narrow coastal plain. To the east was the sea and to the west were the mountains, not one of them as tall as the one which towered above the village itself. That was Mynydd Gareg Wen. It was called Mynydd Gareg Wen — Mountain of the White Rock — because every morning when the sun rose over the sea and cast its light upon the mountain a huge flat rock at the very top of it shone white. It wasn't really white at all but a pale bluish grey, slate grey, though no one knew that because no one dared to climb the mountain and find out.

The people of the village were content enough, but for the presence of the mountain above them, for they had everything to meet their needs. Fishermen went out to sea and caught herring, dabs, mackerel and sometimes quantities of sprats. Cocklewomen scoured the shore at dawn and carried their wares from door to door in wide baskets which they balanced on their heads. Each house had its plot where cabbages, potatoes, turnips, leeks and all manner of garden crops grew in abundance. Some of them kept chickens out the back or a pig in a sty and those who didn't bought from the local farmer, whose milk churns would clank each morning as his daughter Molly, with the horse and cart, took milk to fill the jugs held out at each back door. But they all had a terrible fear, felt and unspoken, amongst them. They feared what lurked on the other side of Mynydd Gareg Wen ...

And so on. An elaborate story where the heroine was Morfydd, a little girl full of curiosity about the world around her, especially at night when she would want both answers to her questions and the prolonging of her mother's warm presence at her bedside. *How does a clock work, mam? How does a snowdrop know when to push its green shoot through the cold earth? Can worms see? How do the stars shine?* — before she was obliged to say her prayers (in my best Welsh!) and go to sleep. Plenty of story, in the Welsh accents of my childhood companions

47

(heavily laced with recollections of childhood experiences, like opening the back door more than once to a woman made tall as a giant's wife by the load of cockles balanced on her head) before she finally reaches the giant and cups her hands around him ...

O, cariad! Dew, wyt ti buchgen bach! There's a little, little thing you are!

... and finds out who he is. And the teenagers have listened, still as sculptures of themselves, caught up from first to last in a fairy story I would tell to 4-year-olds, which they had already heard in brief moments before I went Welsh on them.

I had been asked by their teacher to encourage these young people to tell stories orally and, if possible, persuade the few bilingual pupils present to incorporate their home languages in their storytelling. My Welsh version was my route to those ends. During the next lesson the pupils worked in groups to follow my instructions: *take the simple story and elaborate it in a version which puts the events in a new setting, perhaps a place familiar to you like Wales is to me, and try to include some language or dialect that is different from what is spoken round here. That's if you can. And change anything you want in the story, of course.*

I am now the proud possessor of a videotape made by a colleague of the English teacher concerned which shows what those people made of the story. The very first group which chose to demonstrate their skills in front of the class were three girls, one of whom turned out to have enormous talents as a storyteller, which provided an eloquent start for the other two, who included Bengali spoken between mother and daughter in the tale and Punjabi spoken between the giant and the girl who found him. This was the first time either of the girls, the only pupils of Asian origin in the class, had ever brought their bilingual skills to anyone else's notice.

And the English advisers I referred to earlier did pretty well with the story, too. So did a group of remarkable primary and secondary teachers from Cheshire, where I went with my husband to work with them for a day. Whole day stints mean that there is room for practical work in which the participants can enjoy both oral and written storytelling, and to share both real-life and make-believe sequences — in so far as one can make claim to a division between the two, that is.

On this particular occasion, having told them my 'Welsh' version of *The Giant over the Mountain* and talked about my experiences telling this tale, I suggested they write a version of the story for themselves for their own satisfaction, or perhaps in a form suitable for telling to their own pupils, or — I said — "You might fancy writing a story which picks up the main message, relating it — or not, as you wish — to something from your own experience". Plenty of choice there and plenty of time to mull it over and do the writing. After those 'instructions' we had lunch around 1 o'clock and pooled the written results at about 3 p.m.

I have two abiding legacies from the ensuing portion of the afternoon. One was a version which comes into the last category of my suggestions, *The Giant Injection* (see Part 3, page 158) a piece which would make welcome reading in any upper primary or secondary classroom. It was read out to the whole group — as luck would have it (I always grieve over the work I never hear or see on such occasions!) — and I remembered the author's name was Carol, so it was not difficult at a later date to track her down for my present enterprise.

Alas, the other piece has gone forever as far as I am concerned though not, I hope, unused by the author herself or her infants. Infants, yes. At the sharing time of that day I joined one of the dozen or so groups and listened with as much pleasure as the others to the different offerings. Somehow I knew which one of the group would be last to contribute. I'd done much peeping around at the participants during the writing (I was doing my own account of a giant-in-the-mind bully from my own childhood) and noticed her among the totally busy, silent throng. She had arrived that day without a companion and had remained alone, as far as I had observed, all day. Though seated at the front she had made no contributions during discussions and had asked no questions. Some of the teachers seemed to be furiously writing without pause during the whole hour of the allotted time but she seemed to stare into space just as much as she put pen to paper. She didn't appear to be anxious, just tentative, perhaps; thoughtful; a bit separate.

We all turned to her expectantly but she didn't begin reading. Instead, she said something like, "I just want to say that this is the first time I have ever read anything to adults. I'm not used to this kind of writing at all. I've had to write it as I might tell it to the children in my class. You see I am only a reception class teacher …" I heard no more but am aware that we all made encouraging noises and body-language to get her started on the job which she did.

Inwardly I was spluttering with rage at whatever combination of circumstances, most of which we know or can easily guess, had led her to be so self-effacing — apologetic! — over her professional role. How few of us who call ourselves teachers could cope all day with her intake of tiny people, ones who arrive in the first place ignorant of and incompetent in all the skills essential to a school agenda, all those basic skills, not least the social ones, which are taken for granted in older pupils by their teachers. How few secondary staff would willingly, still less successfully, swop places with her! And would they ever learn to do well such a genuinely giant job? Only this week I was reading in the *Times Educational Supplement* an article about the assessment of infants written by a senior adviser (no less) which began thus:

I intended to spend the best part of a day with a class of 5-year-olds embarking on their National Curriculum careers with a teacher new to both. I lasted the morning. My background in secondary schools had not prepared me for the persistence of infants, for the squabbles and short attention spans, for their inability to blow their own noses or tie shoelaces.

At least he was honest about his professional inferiority to the teacher he had come to advise!

This particular reception class teacher started reading. I shall not attempt to reproduce the delicacy, precision and unsentimental tenderness with which she told her tale. Instead I will tell you about her version of *The Giant over the Mountain*. She began with her giant, alone and unloved, in a cave far from the bustle of human activity in the valley below. Suddenly there were the voices of children near by, calling to each other, one persuading, the rest fearful, but not so fearful as the giant himself because he knew they would be shocked by the sight of such an ugly creature as himself, for he was totally bald and covered with warts. A little girl draws near and greets him. A conversation takes place in which she tries to lure him out of his hiding place and down to join in the merriment she shares with her friends. But how could he, he insists, being absolutely bald? She tells him that where she lives there are many fine birds who often shed their feathers: she could collect brightly-coloured feathers and get some glue from her mother's drawer, return and stick the feathers to his head to make him thus beautiful. And that is what happened. But what, the giant insists, can be done about the warts? Her next trip is to fetch some special cream which her mother keeps on the dressing table in her bedroom — which duly does the trick. The giant goes down to the village and fits in a treat ...

At this point it seemed as though the story was finished — its author certainly stopped reading — and I was torn between admiration for her ingenious tale and its appropriateness for her infants in so many ways (just imagine the follow-up work, in words and paint and cardboard and feather!) on the one hand, and doubt about material that was patently baldist and wartist!

She stopped reading, as I have reported to you, and then looked speculatively into the distance just as I'd watched her doing earlier. "I wasn't really happy about how this might affect the children's view of warts and baldness," she said, "so I think I'll finish the story by making the feathers gradually fall off as time goes by, and the warts come back — but of course it wouldn't matter because by then the giant is loved by everybody for what he is and so they don't see the warts ... and so on."

Don't you think a clever reception class teacher is among the *crème de la creme* of the teaching force?

FOOTNOTE: Thanks to the efforts of David Horner (see page 58) who convened the Cheshire workshop, the author of *The Bald, Warty Giant* was tracked down eventually and she kindly agreed to let me have what she produced on that occasion (see Part 3, page 156). Compare her original version with mine from memory above: stories certainly imprint themselves thoroughly!

Chapter 8
EXPLORING PERSONAL EXPERIENCE

Around the time I was sallying forth into other people's classrooms I was also giving talks and running workshops for teachers. There were in-service days, advisers' courses, meetings of the National Oracy Project, an Inner City conference, national and local meetings of NATE (the National Association of Teachers of English) — all concerned at last with oral narrative. Such invitations usually began with a claxon from our telephone just when I'd slammed the front door behind me (my doorkey is under the debris at the bottom of my handbag's clutter) or when the cheese sauce is beginning to thicken in the pan. I grew to hate the calls that were not followed up by a confirmatory letter with all appropriate details included as I am not at my best on the phone to strangers. This is characteristic:

It's a woman's voice:

- Is that Betty Rosen? Yes? Oh, my name is ...

(I lost that bit. My mind was hearing the sound of the person, wondering about it. I'm hopeless when it comes to names. Names actually matter, especially on the telephone or when I'm being introduced to someone — which is just the very moment when the name dissolves. Faces stay. I wish faces came with phone calls ...)

- We would like you to give a talk at Merryott School. It's in Surrey. The first day of term, September 5 ...

(She's got a Welsh accent.)

- ... in-service day, a full day. It's really aimed at ...

- Excuse me, what did you say your name is?

- Sandra Temple. We'd really like you to give the opening talk.

(That's not a Welsh name. Where's the pencil gone?)

- It's really aimed at raising staff awareness about language. If you would be willing ...

(South Wales. Somewhere between Swansea and Ystrad. A valley voice. Not far up the valley, mind.)

- ... ever so pleased. I've read your book. I got straight into it, the first part, the autobiographical part, without stopping. You see, I come from Ponty, from Pontardawe.

- Pontardawe? Well, there's a thing! Pontardawe! ...

And we went on to talk a very lot about Pontardawe and a very little about giving in-service talks to teachers.

Yes, I remember Ponty all right. We caught a little fat James bus to it or a double decker United Welsh, which ran along the main road from Swansea to Ystradgynlais, getting on at the Mond stop in Clydach where I lived out my childhood and adolescence. Three miles from Clydach it was; nine miles from Swansea. That was the only road to Pontardawe for regular traffic, running alongside the Tawe river and the canal. Footsloggers could get to Ponty along the canal tow path. I walked that way with my mother when I was only little ... (see Part 3, page 166).

One is so much more articulate and entertaining when sharing recollections from past experience, as Sandra and I did that day, than talking business; than talking anything else at all, for that matter, with the single exception of matters of the immediate moment. Our memories make storytellers of us all. The storyteller is everywhere. She sits with her tea cup in her hand, or her coffee or cocktail or pint of bitter. She leans, laughing into the phone. She squats on the edge of the bed before Morfydd goes to sleep. Her tongue will busy itself when she comes home after her operation or when she visits her mum in December for Christmas turkey, or in November for Divali. In the office lunch hour on Monday she will pause between bites of her sandwich to relate her Saturday night. Tales to a stranger can relieve the monotony of a bus or supermarket queue.

Stories are where all good talk is.

Yes, I settled down with my memories of Ponty much more readily and willingly than I tackled the preparation of that in-service occasion. By the same token, a relaxed classroom will elicit more joy in the recall of the personal past than in the recall of any taught data or the performance of a formal exercise. The texture of our own culture is the weave of our own stories, for teacher and pupil alike. When we look back as adults, the detail of our past events may have undergone a sea change in the course of recollecting, many times over during the years between; such is the process of any story re-telling. Yet, oddly, I find certain facts — for instance, the names of persons as far back as primary school classmates and teachers — will skip off my tongue more speedily than the names of pupils and colleagues from my last place of work, or those of the new neighbours.

Part and parcel of classroom interchange involves pupils' recollections of past events, and we teachers who concern ourselves with the language development of our pupils encourage such reminiscences. I would argue in this context that what is right for our pupils is also right for ourselves. While indulging in the very same activity we share its fruits.

Let me suggest some of the benefits of spending time on the backward glance.

Without memory there is no identity. In the words of Oliver Sacks from *The Man who Mistook his Wife for a Hat* :

> *If we wish to know about a man, we ask "what is his story — his real, inmost story?" — for each of us is a biography, a story. Each of us is a singular narrative, which is constructed, continually, unconsciously, by, through, and in us — through our perceptions, our feelings, our thoughts, our actions; and, not least, our discourse, our spoken narrations. Biologically, physiologically, we are not so different from each other; historically, as narratives — we are each of us unique.*

> *To be ourselves we must have ourselves — possess, if need be re-possess, our life stories. We must 'recollect' ourselves, recollect the inner drama, the narrative, of ourselves. A man needs such a narrative, a continuous inner narrative, to maintain his identity, his self.*

We are nothing if not the accumulation of our memories, therefore they must have status in the classroom if pupils are to operate with self-respect. It is individual identity which we are most particularly concerned with in the classroom. In the expression of it, the pupil is likely to be at his or her most articulate. Fluency breeds fluency. This way, standards of achievement are met.

Recollecting involves coming to terms with not only ourselves but also that part of ourselves which derives from parents and grandparents whose own recollections become part of our past scene. These are the people (along with our peers, our neighbours, our schoolteachers etc.) who have created the environment that shaped us. They in their turn were shaped by their forebears, and so the whole family culture establishes itself around the individual. A veritable maze of separate items become relevant to the flavour of this culture, ranging from major issues of ideology to the little fact, in my own case, that along the canal bank to Ponty my mum and I noshed fairy cakes with glacé cherries on, rather than mango or jalebi or haman taschen or halva … It is fun to itemise these things but also crucial if the child's culture is to enter with her through the school gates. Doing so we, as teachers, will assist the pupils in locating the particulars of their experience, make it safe and acceptable for them to do so and, without a doubt, oil the wheels of the working day for everyone concerned.

At a more subtle level, we need the self-knowledge which arrives in the course of recollecting. It is as valuable to assess our own nature and disposition through past events. In looking back we observe ourselves in action. We know what we did and why. However uninspiring our behaviour has been, we must struggle with explanations while inevitably empathising with the self that has long sunk into the abyss of time. This process is part of a continuum without which the individual cannot hope to face present and future contingencies with any confidence.

We filter out of the past the symptoms of our present identity. We wonder about what has slipped through our memory's fingers, not to mention what never was but might have been:

A Ball

Laura laughs
if she sees a ball bounce

I don't think it's funny

I wonder if
I used to laugh
at a ball bouncing
when I was two
like Laura.

If I used to laugh
why did I stop?

Michael Rosen

My Ponty memories are innocuous indeed but it is not always so. There are stories of the past that hurt. There are stories which pluck up guilt or shame or pain, which only the most courageous will tell, and even then perhaps only to themselves.

They all matter.

Our identity is made up of an amalgam of those past experiences, right up to the present and into the imagined future. To make sense of ourselves, for ourselves, not only do we select from our memories but we invent beginnings and endings for them which do not exist as such in the continuous flow of our own living. Thus the storyteller inside each head constructs the tale. When we look forward in time, trying to envisage events to come, we visualise how things might be in the light of what we already know, projecting sequences on the future, glamourising possible high spots and catastrophising possible obstacles and dangers. We might even actually picture the sequence of that most convincing of artificial endings of Time — our own death. We may do so for someone else: certainly every mother who has experienced the crisis of an offspring's failure to come home on time, or his avoidance of the telephone and mailbox while trekking in distant parts of the globe, will tell herself a terrible tale or two of final disaster too horrible in narrative particulars to be put into words. What if ... is the once upon a time of the tales we invent for ourselves in mental autobiography. We think in stories manufactured out of what we already know. Story is the tool with which we reflect, calculate, speculate.

Our autobiographies matter. Such stories must be told — in the head, with the tongue and on paper. We are all, *all* storytellers. Such was my first message to the people at Merryott School and at several more in-service workshops — but not in such words! I simply tell them stories. Of Ponty. Or of somewhere else in the localities of my past. Then they tell each other stories, wonderful stories, many, many stories. What follows is a sample of such testimony.

Chapter 9
AUTOBIOGRAPHICAL STORYTELLING

THE SCHOOL CAP

This is a tape transcript of a story told by David Horner, a Yorkshireman, at a NATE conference workshop, 1989.

I'd never had to wear a school uniform before, but once I'd passed that 11-plus that meant I'd spend the next seven years going to school in nothing but school uniform. At first I was so excited at the prospect and so proud that I could wear clothes that would show where I was going and where I belonged. I used to pester my mum once I'd bought it to allow me to go out in the streets with it before the school year began or go and play in the park in it and show it off to my friends there. Well, of course, she'd hear none of that, insisting that it stayed in the wardrobe until the school year began.

I seem to remember on the very last evening when I went to play in the park, a warm September evening before school was to begin the next day, I did manage to sneak the belt out and threaded it through my trousers and went off to play. My friends were in fact quite rude about it when they saw it and they weren't impressed at all. They said things like, "Ey, he's a Grammar bug! a Bluebottle!"

Well, the next day came and I can still see the picture that my mum took of me in the early autumn sunlight with my new school bicycle, a bicycle which, when we bought it in Curry's, my mum had insisted that the handlebars were changed. She'd said to the man that drop-handlebars were very dangerous and in any case all parents of children going to the grammar school had had a letter personally from the headmaster saying that he didn't approve of drop-handlebars because it made young gentlemen from the school appear to ride bicycles in undignified positions. So there I was, with my bike, with its straight handlebars, in my new school uniform: short trousers, blazer, long socks, shining black shoes, and my school cap trim on my head.

Sometime on that first day there must have been an assembly, an assembly for just the new boys of the school. A Mr Green, who was the teacher in charge of the first year, had got us all together to tell us about what we would expect to get from life at the school and what the school would expect of us. He told us that we had to work hard, that the good name of the school lay with us. And when it came to the matter of uniform he said, "You are either IN uniform or OUT of it. If you are OUT of uniform you do not wear ANY of your school uniform."

I was glad he hadn't seen me in the park the night before.

"If you are IN school uniform you wear it ALL and you must be neat and tidy. Wear it with PRIDE."

I did. I was very proud of my school uniform.

"If you see a teacher when you are out in the town," continued Mr Green, "I want you to greet that teacher properly. No crossing over the street pretending you haven't seen them. No sniggering and giggling in doorways. No mumbling. You say GOOD MORNING or GOOD AFTERNOON or GOOD EVENING and you raise your cap to the teacher. Raise your cap, by the peak, as a mark of respect."

Now one thing I'd better tell you about my school. Not only was it a grammar school but it also had some pupils who were boarders, and because of that we had no lessons on a Wednesday afternoon. On a Wednesday afternoon, if you wanted to, you could join the CCF — Combined Cadet Force — and play at soldiers for the afternoon. But it also meant you had to have lessons on a Saturday morning. I couldn't wait to get started. And on Wednesday afternoons I would keep my school uniform on and I would go out into the town, teacher hunting.

One Wednesday afternoon I couldn't believe my luck. I saw, coming towards me down a busy street in the centre of town, not just a teacher from the school, but Mr Green, the teacher in charge of the first year, the teacher who had told us how to behave — and I DID know how to behave. When he got near to me, I looked him straight in the eye and I said, "Good afternoon, Mr Green," and I raised my cap by the peak and walked on by.

The next morning in school assembly there was the usual hymn, and the usual notices, and a boy from the sixth form in a different coloured blazer read a part from the Bible. And Mr Green had a special notice. He said, "There was a boy yesterday who greeted me in town. A member of the first year, I think. I should like to see that boy, at my study, immediately after this assembly."

It was me he meant, I was sure of it. There may have been other boys but I had made a special effort. I was sure he meant me. So I whispered to my friend that

I'd be a bit late and to tell the teacher whose lesson I was due at that I was speaking with Mr Green and I went along and I waited outside Mr Green's study.

Eventually Mr Green came along. "Er ... Mr Green?"

"Yes, boy?"

"You wanted to see me."

Clearly he didn't remember me. Well, that was only to be expected; he must see a lot of boys.

"I'm the boy, Mr Green, the boy who greeted you in town yesterday."

"Ah, yes. I think I do recognise you. Come into my study."

His voice was stern and cold. But I went in. And he sat down at a large desk and made me stand in front of it. I felt terribly, terribly small but I knew he was going to say something quite wonderful to me.

"What do you think you were playing at?" said Mr Green.

"I'm sorry ...?"

"Yesterday afternoon. What do you think you were doing, behaving in that impertinent manner?"

"But ... but I ..."

"What do you think you were playing at? Tell me what you did!"

"I saw you, Mr Green, and I did what you said, you said if we saw a teacher from the school we ought to greet them properly ..."

"Yes, and do you think that was properly? Raising your cap in that ridiculous and insulting fashion?"

"But I raised it by the peak, Mr Green, as you said ..."

"Have you got your school cap with you, boy?"

I had. It was neatly folded inside my satchel.

"Take it out. Put it on your head."

I took it out. I put the cap on my head.

"Show me what you did yesterday afternoon."

I lifted my arm and I took my cap from my head by the peak.

"You're doing it again, you stupid boy! What do you think you are doing?"

"I … I'm raising my cap by the pea …"

"That is not the peak!" said Mr Green. "That is the peak! What you raised it by was the button!"

The button …? Surely that was the peak of the cap, the top of the cap, like the peak of a mountain. I couldn't understand what he was saying. He'd pointed to a part of the cap and called it the peak that was … the tippy. We called that the tippy in my house. My dad wore a flat cap to go to work and when he went on long walks. And he called it a tippy cap.

"That is how you raise a cap, you silly boy!"

I stared at Mr Green. I stared at the cupboards that surrounded him, full of dark books behind glass-windowed doors. I grew cold all over and I can remember the tears welling up and bursting down over my cheeks.

GRASS

A tape transcript of a story told by George Murphy of Halifax at a workshop on Storytelling, 1989, Leeds.

I was trying to draw a horse on the living room door but it kept coming out as scribble. Each time I rubbed it out with the cuff of my sleeve then, ponderously, as if trying out a new limb, I downstroked a curved blue line. A horse's fore-leg appeared. I pressed on a wedge of torso, three more legs bent contrariwise into a gallop, a strong neck and, lifting my own chin in equine affinity, a proud horse's head. A blue stallion galloped across a creamy plain. I signed off with a flourish of tail.

I walked portentously outside. We lived in Dunkirk Street, where the ruddy bricked houses opened out to encompass small twin fields. It was a street like an amphitheatre to a small child. I ran on to the nearest field, smacking my backside like a composite Roy Rogers and Trigger.

The heat stopped me. The road at the top of our street was dancing. The sun, the size of a half-sucked sweet, was vibrating with effort. An aeroplane was droning fitfully somewhere as if invisible hands were clamping on and off me ears in that game we sometimes played. I searched the huge sky, too blue for craning, until I saw at last the tiny silver flash, impossibly high. I listened to the plane's intermittent complaints long after it had passed out of view, suggesting the curve of earth beyond the rooftops of Dunkirk Street. Then the other somnolent summer sounds returned. A lawn mower somewhere and the next street's traffic.

Then I heard the twinnies, laughing. The twinnies were playing with Big Clifford on their front lawn. They'd taken all their clothes off. They had hollow backs and little pot-bellies lined with veins like the rivers on a map. Big Clifford leaned over me, his face all red and his ears aflame and said, "Why don't you take your clothes off, George?" So I did.

When I took me underpants off it was like taking off a layer of skin, I felt so bare. Then we danced round the twinnies little garden pretending to be Indians and patting our mouths, shouting, "woowoowoowoowoo!" and Clifford ran after us, laughing. Then Clifford said, "Why don't yous put some grass up your bums?" So we did.

I cropped a wodge of grass from the twinnies trim lawn and tucked it between my buttocks. It tickled. Nicely. Then we ran, ululating wildly and feeling more savage than ever. I spun around and around and around with me arms outstretched and stopped, suddenly, catching the world out. Then it pulled me down to the ground and the twinnies fell, laughing, too.

Then we heard our itchy gate scrape open. We dived for cover behind the twinnies variegated privet. Between the bare legs of the hedge I could see me mum. She was walking down our path. When she got to top of our path she shouted, "Geo — orge! Yer dinner's ready!"

The twinnies snorted with suppressed laughter and me and Clifford had to hit at them to be quiet.

My mum surveyed the shimmering street. Then she shouted again. "Geo — orge! Yer dinner's ready!"

The street was silent in reply. I could see me mum's face and how worried she looked. I wanted to run out to her and shout, "It's all right, Mum. Here I am!"

But I couldn't because I was stark naked with grass up me bum.

Both of these stories I transcribed from tapes produced after the occasions when I first heard them. The second story has all the flavour of literary rather than oral discourse, especially during the first portion when George, all alone, interacts with the world around him before the activities of his neighbours impinge upon his privacy. Yet it *was* a told story. I heard it. I remember how each face in front of George (and me) drifted into the mood of his hot afternoon. I remember how we all fell about with laughter, over the garden goings-on. I remember someone saying later, "What did you mean, 'the sky too blue for craning'?" — a thought which a reader would savour rather than question. I remember the cat-calls and ribald remarks tossed out from the audience, casting doubt upon the integrity of Big Clifford; and I remember George laughing back, assuring everyone that hindsight made him inclined to share their response. It was a totally oral occasion.

And I remember that occasion well, uniquely for me, because it took place not very long ago. But for George the performance was the ultimate of many retellings of certain events which had occurred two or three decades previously. For him, this meant many years of recollection, of revisioning, embellishing, explaining, assessing, polishing, shaping, metaphor-making, forgetting, and remembering memories. And George, like most teachers, is steeped in a literary culture. Hardly surprising, then, that in the midst of, because of, in spite of, an international resurgence of oral narrative, some of us tell our stories without any desire to shake off what the written word has done to and for us in our lives.

Not only does our literary experience affect how we speak and think but it allows us the luxury of recording our own narratives in written form, shaped by whatever leisurely reflection we may require.

Earlier I tried to transmit something of the spirit of my daughter's place of work: "Rosalind's nursery" as I have come to refer to it among friends. Unlike her sister who, as the only female service advisor for a prestigious UK car manufacturing firm, earns more at the age of 23 than I did as a senior teacher in a comprehensive school, Rosalind earns tuppence. It upsets me to think how little financial reward there is for the kind of vital socio/educational work she does, as teachers do, with all the stresses attached. When I talk to her about this she always finishes up by saying how much she cares for the children and insists that rewards are intrinsic to her contact with them.

I have no doubt that another essential ingredient, in addition to actually liking little children, which goes towards success in dealing with infants is a sense of humour. Rosalind has never been short of that. I recollect a camping holiday in France when, with Rosalind at 11 months in a carrier on my back, we 'did' a series of chateaux along the Loire. In one of them we entered a room full of life-sized portraits. To the chagrin of Monsieur le Guide, each single one elicited from my baby an instant drawing in of breath, a pause, then peels of tinkling laughter which echoed against the high ceiling to the exclusion of all other sounds, notably those the guide was trying to make. Just what she found so funny is a matter for speculation but the laughter has stayed with her over her two decades and usually its a more communal activity than it was on that occasion long ago. I quote below an extract from a diary/log book she keeps; you'll see what I mean.

MINE'S CALLED A TOTEE

By Rosalind Watson, child-care worker.

... In the middle of the cleaning-up job I started thinking about an occasion during my own days at nursery school when I wet my knickers, leaving a puddle which steadily grew and spread across the parquet flooring. I felt I ought to cry for my wickedness yet instead I just watched it disperse. The teacher lent me a pair of knickers which had a picture on the front of them. Mine never had any pictures on and they all turned grey in the wash and had dangling bits of thread which tickled my legs. But my borrowed knickers were magnificent and I didn't want to give them back. Needless to say they were returned without question ...

"When I am big I'm going to school," Shanelle tells me, distraught at the idea that her year older brother will get there before her. I am surrounded by children who have a longing for school unaware of the hurt that I and my co-workers feel each time they joke that they won't visit us when they leave. Will they remember the time when they wet their pants at nursery or will it be more positive goings-on?

There was that trip to Margate we organised for the kids and their parents. All my key children came with their parents so I planned a nice free day with my mum and my sister who had come along with us. Before long I had acquired Shanelle and Candice on our travels — their parents were either taking a well earned break or grabbing the chance to go on the more daring rides at the funfair. We headed for the beach and on our arrival Shanelle looked around in total disbelief. She had never seen such a huge sandpit and, as if her legs had given way, she fell towards the sand and set to playing immediately. Candice was less confident. She was reluctant to walk on it as though she expected it to swallow her up. We moved on slowly across the sand through the sunbathers towards our group. I carried Candice some of the way, trying to convince her it was safe but she was still dubious. Shanelle on the other hand was in the distance with my mum. They were having to sit down every few yards so that Shanelle could sit down and have a ritual sand-feel. When we reached the others Candice cuddled up and we both tucked into some Greek cheese someone had brought. Shanelle sat endlessly playing with the sand. It was her first time on a beach. Would she look through the nursery book At the Seaside in a different way now she had experienced it for herself? Would she expect our next trip to be a visit to Goldilocks and the three bears or to outer space? Had she realised that seaside was real and not just fantasy? Shanelle still talks about the trip to the seaside and how she came with me, my mum, *my sister and Candice — and that we had gone into a cafe for a drink, even remembering what drinks we all had ...*

She still questions me about things we did that day and much more besides. The children feel at ease questioning. Eating-time is a favourite for their serious discussions and often they seem to ponder a great deal before finding the courage to speak their minds. Suzanne turned to Andrew one day. "Your mum's big," she says. Andrew acts as if he's not interested so she repeats, "Your mum's big, isn't she, Andrew?"

Andrew drops what he's doing and looks up thoughtfully.

Suzanne, plucking up courage from Andrew's lack of aggression, adds "She's fat, isn't she, Andrew?"

Very doubtfully Andrew agrees. "Yes, she is."

"Well, you'd better watch out," comes the reply, "because one day she might go pop goes the weasel."

I was fit to bust but the children just listened with interest and proceeded with their dinner. I wondered how long Suzanne had wanted to tell Andrew her thought and had waited for the right moment to come out with it.

One teatime I gave all the children a pile of raisins each. Natalie looked at her plate in total disbelief. She prodded the raisins. She looked across at me then down at her plate. With great consideration she asked, "Did you get these from the rabbit?" Obviously she had seen what our rabbit had left dotted about the garden and had taken for granted that the same items were on her plate. What would have happened if she had not asked her question? Would she have gone home with dire stories about the effect of council cuts?

Yet how far can the children question me? How much am I able to respond freely without the parents' agreement?

One day one of the children started chatting about 'boobs'. On the television the night before there had been the premiere of **Airplane 2**. *She had understood from it that breasts were nothing more than showpieces. My co-worker explained to her that they were not boobs but breasts and went on to explain their function. For weeks afterwards she was obsessed with the idea. "Breasts" she'd say, and comment upon whether they were big or small. This became embarrassing as I am not well endowed on this front. She'd quite happily take a handful of my breast and say, "Little breast". This left me in a* humiliating predicament. We eventually mentioned the matter to her mum and the phantom breast-grabber gave up her endeavours.

Queries about breasts can be answered but what about those other taboo parts of the body which, when we are dealing with the under-5s, we prefer to forget? What do we call those portions? My automatic answer would be — a boy has a willie and a girl has a ...? Although a parent may not hesitate when it comes to saying 'willie' to a son, often there is a special name for a daughter's. That makes it difficult for me. I've decided mine is a totee which is what my boyfriend's mum called it when he was small though strictly this was a unisex name. One day Charlene, who had been told by her mum to call her totee her vagina, was messing about and being silly. I said to her, "You're getting too big for your boots." She looked at me and laughed. "Well, you're getting too big for your vagina." What a dilemma! Should I laugh or begin a lengthy speech headed 'Why my totee is not a laughing matter'? It took me no time at all before I was laughing with everyone else.

Although I have become more experienced with these taboo subjects I'm always open to suggestions. I listen eagerly on a bus or in a queue when I hear a child saying, "Mummy, where do babies come from?" though very often the child is told to be quiet while the parent looks round frantically hoping no one has heard ...

Part 2 TEACHERS' WORKSHOPS

Chapter 1
IRISH TALES, OISIN, AND THE REALM OF MERMAIDS

From real-life experience come such tales and I begin most of my sessions with references to it.

In schools, before providing what everyone is waiting for, I might say, "Has anyone got an Irish granny?" If it happens to be a Catholic comprehensive that's a pretty safe starter. We then move on to the ones who have Italian grannies or grandpas and the hows and the whys of it. One can often *see* those who have African, Caribbean or Asian forebears but I tend to save them up: most societies are racist enough to make such people reticent about their grannies and grandads, unless everybody around is united in a shared recognition of such specialnesses — a state of affairs which I can manufacture, for the moment at least, having asked my question. Many more grannies emerge — the Scottish, the Polish, the Devonian, the Northumbrian, the Liverpudlian ... I get them all in. They are all significant — which is one reason for asking the question. The other is that culture-based folk stories are international travellers — and I am in their school because of such stories. Another is that I need an excuse for telling a story with a touch of the Irish in my voice (my having a granny from Dublin), a facility acquired not from ethnicity or residency but from hours of listening to my closest friend who is Irish, and hearing the sounds of it from John Cole and other reporters and weather forecasters on television. Having established that cultural diversity is a treat which we should make the most of, I tell them about the Irish granny who sat me on her knee and told me stories ... well, maybe she didn't but it makes a good story. And a convenient start.

But with adults it is different. I get straight into the story of *The Fisherman and the Mermaid*. Or the story of Oisin — *Usheen* — yet another being who, like the boy in *The Land where No one ever Dies*, was forbidden to dismount from his horse on pain of death. It's a story which my Irish friend Monica drew to my attention as a result of her reading my version of that Italian story. Usheen, the hunter, drawn by the elusive stag even to a rock in the middle of swirling water, and carried on its back to the land of the ever young, which is under the seven seas or maybe at the other side of the world or maybe even — for a select few of us — in the very here and now. Usheen, like the boy who reaches the place where no one ever dies, longs to return to his own folk once more and attempts it — on horseback. In order to savour again those precious days of kinship he dismounts and shrivels to dust (See Part 3, Page 171). Read it now — it is always better to encounter stories than to read about them. And while you're there, read *The Fisherman and the Mermaid*, page 174.

I try in these workshops to transmit the power of oral stories so that teachers will give them their rightful place in the classroom. The best way to get this across is, first, to tell a story, knowing they will listen and become as involved as the children do. Often teachers have given up their time at the end of a working day: they then deserve to be soothed and entertained by a story rather than lectured at so the story begins straight away. Perhaps I will give examples of pupil retellings, from audio or video tapes or from texts, to indicate the quality of work which children produce after listening to a story. If there is more time — at a conference or a day's workshop — I will begin by asking them to tell each other stories from their own lives, knowing everyone will be entertained thoroughly as narrators and listeners: this is an easy route to the realisation that we are all in fact storytellers, transmitting every day of our lives stories and bits of stories and stories by implication; sometimes they contain powerful messages and make compelling listening, like those in the preceding section.

After that, if not sooner, I will tell a story, such as the tale of Usheen. My motive in doing so is to impress on teachers the importance of using this kind of material in the classroom. As such occasions have multiplied, however, another motive has crept in of itself: I want teachers to feel — perhaps for the first time — the excitement of being themselves highly creative inventors through language. I want them to enjoy being the authors they are.

Insofar as we wrest particular meanings out of general systems we are all creators; a speaker is to utterance what an author is to texts.

M Holquist

Thus it is that my workshops have become something much bigger than the promotion of a yet another useful classroom device. For some, and I include myself here, the intrinsic pleasure and the morale boost which follows is enormous and the long-term effects are sustaining to one's self-confidence in the face of whatever may be perpetrated by our masters.

But the process must begin with an Usheen, binding everyone into a unit at the outset. I am anxious only about doing proper justice to the tale itself but not over its impact and subsequent inspiration to creative invention — of the latter I can be one hundred per cent sure. At first I was very nervous about telling stories to adults but that is no longer the case. Unlike most of the children I have taught, an audience of teachers will be respectfully silent in front of a speaker even if they are bored, sceptical or simply daydreaming about something else, but I can spot the difference between polite 'attention' and the utter absorption of an audience of committed listeners. From experience I can now be certain that, whatever happens on either side of it, during the storytelling itself the whole group will be hooked. Thus I taste power! Not so much my own but that of the TOLD tale.

I want to explore now the results of telling such stories to teachers. Let me state clearly in advance that what emerged has been as exciting a discovery for me as anything I have experienced previously in decades of school teaching and several years of working in higher education with a mixture of school leavers, graduates and mature students.

In brief, when teachers retell stories in a workshop, orally or in writing, the variety of approach in content, style, mood, is truly amazing. Originality is an inevitability. Individual skill abounds. The richness of each individual past life becomes a resource. In these constraining times, the storytelling workshop becomes a place of release. Let me tell you about it.

BEGINNING WITH A PICTURE

I have always found that the most useful aid to me as a storyteller is a stock of visual images, a series of them, to be called forth as the story progresses. Such mental pictures (for the moment I will adopt the convenient parallel with camera 'stills', though as I will show later this is not in fact an accurate representation of what actually goes on in the head) are more immediately fertile and evocative of the story itself than any text learned by rote. A storyteller is a different animal from an actor, though an actor's skills may perhaps be called upon.

While I am telling a story and verbally presenting my own pictures of the scenes and events, a similar process goes on in the mind of the audience as the story unfolds. Though the images in the mind of each listener are initiated by and dependent upon the words that I speak, the very fact that they are occurring in someone else's head inevitably means that such visions — coming so hot on the heels of my own expression of each one — are different from mine, though almost simultaneously experienced. Whatever reflective assessment may also be going on, concerning the import of the story as a whole or that of any of its parts, these images are uppermost in the imagination of the listener — essentially created from the catalytic words of the teller.

I remember hearing Arthur Miller, in a television interview based on his autobiography, tell of the total and prolonged silence which followed the first performance of *Death of a Salesman* and how, very, very gradually, people in the audience began to talk quietly together. Massive applause, almost as an irrelevant afterthought when one person's hand-clap reminded all the rest of where they were with conventions attached, did not come until much later. My strong suspicion is that the silence which so often follows a storytelling, whether the listeners are adults or children, is a time when the images of the story are racing across the canvas of the inward eye, flashing about, nudging and ousting each other, one struggling for attention at the expense of another, until, perhaps, the one that has most significance for the individual dominates and takes hold. Quite often I will exploit this suspicion as soon as the silence has become self-conscious. I will tell the audience how important images are to me and ask them to concentrate on ONE particular picture from the story which made an impact upon them. It is such a simple request (relative, for instance, to "What is the story really saying?" at the end of *The Giant over the Mountain*, which makes very different demands, cognitively and linguistically), open-ended and pleasurably accepted. Then I will ask for volunteers to tell which bits they see. Always there are plenty of contributions to share.

Several things are happening at this semi-discussion stage in the proceedings. First, the story is revealed as now being the common property of the whole group rather than something exclusive to the storyteller. Second, there is a general mulling-over as people are reminded of different portions of the story when specific moments in it

71

are referred to — if you like, it's a bit of classroom 'revision'! This is useful for ensuring that the feel of the story is maintained into the next phase of the workshop. But most important of all, the listeners, who have been apparently passive during the telling, are thus explicitly established as a body of individual initiators of narrative. Inevitably, without exception, every such occasion gives rise to fresh, elaborated representations of moments from the story, even though the speakers *set out merely to restate the words they actually heard.*

If the fancy takes me, or my time is short (perhaps my session with the teachers is limited to 1½ hours or less), I need go no further than this before making the next move which is to invite people to produce their own re-tellings of the story, or at least to begin doing so. When more time is available, there would be discussion of other aspects of the story and any issues raised within it. At this point I could provide the group with a list of some of the very many ways in which a reteller might change a story (see pages 73–5) but enough is enough: to present a plethora of routes would make for confusion or — worse! — an uncomfortable reaching for change for the sake of change. Then people fuss over the task and the unwelcome questions start popping up: "Is it all right if I ...?", "Do you want us to ...?" which call forth an irritable "You must do whatever pleases you!" from me as I realise I've not been clear enough in my preamble. My aim is that each person achieves a retelling which has emerged as easily as possible out of his or her genuinely felt perceptions of the story.

I will suggest that each participant in the workshop forgets everybody else and gets inside him or herself to reconstruct the story simply by giving it a new starting point. This new beginning should (I say) take the shape of one particular visual moment from the story, such as one of those which have been referred to in the prior discussion. What results is a wonderful variety of beginnings — much wider, I may add, than the purely 'visual' sort on which I am concentrating now.

This part of the proceedings may have to last a very short while if time presses. "Think about how you would start," I say; minutes pass; "Right, now tell the person sitting next to you your beginning, and vice versa. Take care, though — you are now the storyteller so don't talk ABOUT your beginning but BEGIN." This is enough to give everyone a taste of what retelling stories means. The full impact of it comes through, however, when more time is available for richer, more considered openings, whether oral or in writing.

Alas, the oral tellings have left me, apart from a few which I have caught on audio tape, but I have many, many written pieces. Some are neatly done or even sent to me later in typed script but most are on torn-out sheets and scraps of paper, containing surprisingly few signs of hesitation or deletion. All speak from the page of their author's spontaneous, enthusiastic involvement. I have plenty, then, to choose from to use here as examples, so I must find representative samples — a frustrating task since every one that I possess is well worth reading. As part of the inevitable selection process, I am confining myself to just two stories, of Usheen, and the mermaid tale; and, for the moment, the beginnings only, acquired by the process I have described above.

First, by way of contrast, a very straightforward picture to open the Usheen story, written by a an under-achieving 14-year-old boy, to show the very least that can be achieved by someone who wants to please and, having been moved into it by the power of the story, feels he is able to.

A crumpled old man lay moaning on the floor by a shining water trough. A white horse which stood by him slowly turned and trotted then galloped away into the distance. The past week flashed before him, he remembered back to the beginning of it all.

A glance at the ending of my version of this story (page 173) will show that even this brief scene contains fresh elements: it is a wide-angled shot which includes the horse; there is a new, effective choice of words e.g. *crumpled*; sound is incorporated directly (*moaning*) and by implication (*trotted, galloped*). The first sentence, though consciously and dramatically 'descriptive', is a simple statement while the second, a more complex one (a subordinate clause, three main verbs) stretches the reader towards the unknown by its form, rhythm and meaning, in anticipation of whichever of the infinity of possibilities for the story's continuation will be chosen by the newly launched teller. An English teacher would be glad to read such words at the start of any pupil's narrative assignment. It is certainly a more striking opening than mine. An underachieving performer, such as this one was according to his teacher who knew him well, could easily be persuaded that composing such a passage was no accident but actually symptomatic of his literary potential.

We, however, are not reluctant learners aged 14 but English teachers, primary teachers or teachers concerned in one capacity or another with language development. We are among those who have succeeded in the educational system to become leaders within it. We have grown up, and we are not short of language. We tell others to compose stories but unwittingly deprive ourselves of the experience, generally speaking. Here is a sample of the word pictures which such teachers can paint and have done so in the kind of workshop I have described. My selection is from a collection of possible openings of *The Fisherman and the Mermaid* at a meeting for primary, secondary English and ESL teachers:

Opening 1

Full moon. A beach. Jagged rock. A calm, empty, empty sea. Shush, shush went the waves and the moonlight danced along them as they wriggled up the sands. Shush, shush they went, again and again and again. If you had been there you would have said that those were the only sounds to be heard and if you'd have looked around you'd have been sure there wasn't a person to be seen or the ghost of a person. All was as empty as a landscape in a dream. But don't go yet. Look out to sea again. As your eyes grow accustomed to the glitter of the moonlight in the still water you see, or you think you see, in the very midst of the band of moonlight a tiny stir. You strain to make sure but no, you were wrong — the water's untroubled. Nothing breaks the surface. Or if it did, it was only for one little moment.

Opening 2

She gazed into the little room. Shadows of the peat fire flickered on the wall. The light glanced off the shiny pans on the dresser. She turned towards the man in his rough clothes and held out her hands, pleading. "Where is my magic garment, fisherman? Would you have me lost in your world?"

"Your sweet song led me to you and now your sea cloth is safe with me. It is clear you were meant to spend your days in this place. Please stay."

"Fisherman, you know I have no choice without my magic garment." For the first time she felt dry warmth on her skin instead of the cool moisture of the waves and the mermaid shivered, half in fear, half in wonderment.

Opening 3

The fisherman had a particular spot amongst the rocks which fringed the sand. Here he would often sit for hours, gazing out beyond the foam-tipped waves to the moonlit horizon. Sometimes he would pick up a handful of pebbles, hurling them into the tip of the foam before it came crashing down onto the glistening sand. And sometimes he would simply sit and cast his mind back over the years to when he was a child, to this same beach, to this same rock and, who knows, perhaps these same pebbles. Half remembered sounds of childish calls came echoing down from the tops of cliffs behind him.

Opening 4

The mermaid had been sitting close to the shore all morning, diving through the waves and surfing along the foam crests, enjoying the sunlight and brisk breeze. She pulled herself on to a rock to rest and bask in the warm sunshine, drying her long golden locks and thinking about her life in the Kingdom of Neptune. She felt sometimes that there was something missing from her life. It could be lonely. To clear away these cloudy thoughts she began to sing softly. As she forgot, her singing grew louder, competing with the crashing of the waves and the bursting of the surf foam. It was as she came to the end of her song that she became aware of a movement in the rocks close by. She felt for her magic garment. It was not there.

Opening 5

In a cool, cool blue green sea-spray dancing light scattered world, deep, deep below the surface of the Atlantic ocean, a world of pale light, eerie luminous dark patches of shadowy mists, a world of swirling, shining lemon green, brown green flowing fronds there lived a mermaid. The walls of her home were lined inside and out with opalescent scales peeled from the interiors of pearly shells. Momentary shafts of light piercing the filmy waters bounced off the scales, met others, creating patterns and movements in a dance. No warmth came from these streaks of light. The deep sea was fresh and tangy. Fish glided past, silently, smoothly. Merfolk rejoiced in this harmonious, peaceful world.

Opening 6

She eased herself on to the flat, moonlit rock and shook the water out of her hair then she spread her magic garment behind her and began to sing. She sang of the sea, the waves and the moon; of the fish and the seals and the sun; of swimming, diving, dipping and soaring through the clear salty water that was her home. Her voice echoed around the rocks and drifted across the white sand.

The fisherman stood without moving, listening and looking at the mermaid on the stone. His eyes slid to the garment that shimmered behind her and his heart began to thud. Without a sound he crept along the cliff path, eased himself gently down the rocks and advanced towards the flat stone the mermaid sang on.

These patently are much more than mere pictures to begin the story! I have been making a conscious pretence in talking of images as though they are stationary paintings. This is not simply a ruse to make my listeners focus on one MOMENT of the action because, when I make up my own 'visual images' in the course of preparing a story for telling, these moments do actually begin for me as static pictures. But as rapidly as thought moves, my pictures become invested with textures, sounds, motion, scents, feelings, attitudes, a past or a future in which feelings and attitudes would be different: invested, in fact, with meaning. If Jack and Jill have a quarrel I see them first, standing half way up the hill glaring at each other; I see Jill's cringing stance before her bully brother; her hair is damply getting into her eyes under the hot sun; I see one of her knee socks round her ankles; I create a hillside and glimpse a landscape beyond which I may or may not work on ... and everything moves from there. Someone else may work a different route, perhaps immediately hearing the words they are flinging at each other: they will work first on dialogue. Perhaps all storytellers find their own quite different routes. All I can say is that choosing an image, a moment, a picture in your mind to begin always seems to work, and it never produces simply a 'visual still'!

Each of these beginnings which I quote has its own distinctive approach while most have preserved the magic, lyrical quality of the story. Most present a mermaid's eye view (although this is not by any means always the case in workshops based around this story — see Part 2, Chapter 3) but the individual focus varies in each — an empty seascape, her song, her play, her ocean floor habitat, etc. The language varies from conversational to the familiar-poetic to the Hopkins-ish *"cool, cool blue green sea-spray dancing light scattered world"*. Here the reader is distanced; in the opening piece, on the other hand, there is a touch of meta-narrative with *"if you had been there"*. And so on.

It is quite clear that each beginning would lead on to a story destined to be very different from any other, not least the story which all these authors shared, word for word, from me. And, I repeat, as a result of nothing more than the injunction to BEGIN IN A DIFFERENT WAY, WITH A MOMENT FROM THE STORY WHICH YOU SEE IN YOUR HEAD.

I hope these openings went on to become complete stories, told in their authors' classrooms. That, after all, is the object of my workshops.

Chapter 2
THE MANY FACES OF RETELLING STORIES

There are so many ways for a reteller to tackle a story. A decade ago, when I first began telling folk tales in my classroom, I made the mistake of coming close to learning texts by heart, especially the purple passages. I know now that if I thoroughly digest the story I will discover my dominant feelings about it. Wrapping these feelings around key moments, I find that the means of retelling comes of itself. Two things I would avoid. One is to try to rote learn the story, which would mean living with the fear of 'getting it wrong', 'it' being someone else's invention. Another is to let whim choose a particular gambit from the kind of list I am about to give you, a list of the things that may possibly be changed when a story is retold. To have authenticity means to be fair to both the story itself and one's own response to it: these should dictate the mode of telling. In this way it is like being true to one's actual experience of the events of the story, so the telling is rather like telling a story from one's own past life — which is the everyday variety of storytelling. One nice effect — which I am sure helps to move me along — is that I believe the story as I'm telling it!

In my workshops I can only do what works for me and I hope will work for others. So far I have, perhaps, been lucky. Another asset is that being open-ended in my demands, people have enough freedom to do what they need to do anyway. Certainly the process I adopt for myself when preparing a story I intend to tell has to be telescoped even if I have several hours with the course members. I rely heavily on the impact of the story I tell. In addition to drawing attention to major 'scenes' in the tale (see previous chapter) I try to identify what issues and themes in it have particularly touched individual members of the group. Such questions as "Whose side do you find yourself on?", "Do you think the ending should be different?", "Does this story have a happy or a sad feel to it?" will bring out the different approaches — as does the initial, apparently uncontentious, request for a favoured image or moment. During the ensuing discussion there is usually a fair measure of disagreement when the points of view of the characters in the story and/or the characters in the workshop come into conflict. All such discussion is valuable. When it's time for individuals to go off and do their own thing with the story, I can safely say, "Try to make your own stance regarding this narrative come through in the way you tell it". Everyone knows what I mean because of what has just taken place.

In *And None of it was Nonsense* (pages 103 — 118) I try to show how the experiences and attitudes which individuals accumulate throughout life profoundly affect the way they retell a story. With such a resource on tap, I find there really is no need for me to do more than I have described here already, as long as my final words are: ABOVE ALL, FEEL FREE TO CHANGE ANYTHING IN IT.

Let me now give you the Rosen list of possible changes which people make — which is by no means exhaustive. It's based on an extract from *Ways of Working with Narrative,* an unpublished paper written in 1986 by Harold Rosen. It might come in useful as discussion material with a class of older pupils by the time they have become accustomed to a storytelling environment in their classroom: a workshop, with stories told, retold, shared and pondered over.

Basically there are three kinds of change.

A Contract

   drop episodes
   drop characters
   reduce or omit description
   omit explanatory comment
   leave point implicit rather than explicit
   omit preamble or moral

B Expand

   invent, or realise more fully, settings and descriptions
   add new incident
   add dialogue
   introduce explicit comment and evaluation
   introduce new characters
   add point, or make existing meanings more explicit
   add invitations to respond

C Substitute

   change characters, their names, associations, meanings (e.g. male to

female)
change the setting
change the point of the story (e.g. making changes to the ending)
tell it from another point of view
change, partly or wholly, from one language or dialect to another
change dialogue
shift the whole style or tone of telling
change one modality to another (e.g. a written story to a spoken one)

This is a very workaday list, which does not distinguish the slight from the fundamental, the casual from the highly considered, the simple (e.g. giving a character a name) from the total (e.g. producing a story which is so different that almost no connection with the stimulus story is detectable, which has occasionally happened during one of my workshop sessions). What is more, it gives no indication of which changes are most likely to occur — which are made most frequently. The changes which a reteller might make look a bit cold-blooded when listed like this, yet such changes may be most subtle, intricate, ingenious and full of feeling in the event. I hope in this exploration of versions of the story of Usheen, which was the starting point of all the scripts I shall use in this section, I shall be able to demonstrate as much.

What emerges is the extraordinary innovative skill of these writers when judged in the ways that good literature is judged anywhere. And I mean all of them, including those whose work I do not quote here. Out of the seventy or so pieces in my possession, I can only think of one which I did not particularly enjoy reading. Even that one, which irritated me because it took the form of a list of rhetorical questions (it was the beginning of a story only because the workshop was short), was somewhat intriguing because of the areas of speculation touched on.

Almost all the writers I am about to quote were primary school teachers. All were invited to make any changes to the story they wished to make.

1 The fuller realisation of specific settings or moments

This is by far the most frequent kind of expansion noticeable when I read through a batch of retellings. Most of the examples given in the previous chapter would fall into this category, though some of them go further in that they involve the invention of new scenes, e.g. the fisherman sitting alone on the beach, thinking about his past; also those writers were more self-consciously 'descriptive' because of the nature of the task set by me. Here, when the writers had freedom to do as they wished, such expansions are situated more naturally in the flow of the tale. While the Usheen story is still — I trust! — fresh in your mind, I shall take my examples in chronological order, as they would have occurred in my version.

The action begins with the day of the hunt; 'on this day' were my words.

Example 1

It happened one golden autumn day when all was rosy and dappled and there was much crackling underfoot in the forest. Usheen and his men were hunting for deer, tracking through dense woods.

Example 2

The sun shone and the blue, blue waters of Galway Bay danced and sparkled on the day O'Sheen and his friends rode out to hunt. A merry day. One that promised well. As they rode through the forest the sound of the horses hooves were muffled upon the ground and the sun and shadows danced around them.

My stag appears — 'a fine beast', 'a great beast'

Example 3

*The stag appeared suddenly from out of the mist enveloping the forest. It was almost evening and the dying rays of the pale winter sun shimmered on the antlers of the magnificent animal, antlers worn proudly with the tips almost touching the lower branches of the trees. The stag, with its royal appearance, was a welcome sight to the weary hunters at the close of a fruitless day …
now it was only a silhouette against the sky …*

… the stag was a powerful swimmer and soon nothing could be seen of him but the tips of his antlers, minute dots on the surface of the water …

[on the second day] the animal seemed to be waiting for them. On their arrival he pawed the ground as if eager for the game to commence.

These are extracts from a long piece in which the author got no further than an argument between the brothers as to which of them would go and wait on the rock. It is a typical illustration of the sort of retelling where all the major events of the story are included but the imagination of the receiver takes the whole thing over and 'relives' it through her own eyes. Inevitably, there will be considerable detail that is new. This is what I find myself doing with stories. This is also what can turn a story into a novel.

My next writer has gone through a similar process. See also from this writer Examples 6 and 10 below.

Example 4

Its antlers were strong and the velvet was nearly rubbed away with only a few ragged ribbons remaining. Its flanks were sleek and shining. It darted through the trees and then tiptoed gracefully through the crackling undergrowth, playing hide-and-seek with the brothers ...

Each day it had reached the edge of the forest, leaping the last few yards across the silvery strip of sand and into the water ... It had stood proudly facing the brothers as if daring them to approach.

Example 5

The huge stag with the golden antlers climbed haughtily onto the rock above the sea.

This was the opening sentence of the retelling. When I read it I was reminded of an ex-pupil of mine, Kevin Als, who took an ordinary mallard out of a story I told (Part 3, page 132) and turned it into a golden duck!

Next, Usheen waits on the rock, "And that he did, silently, with only the soft lapping of the waves for company".

Example 6

He listened — nothing. He waited. The cold of the water began to make him shiver. A watery winter sun came up but he could see nothing. He listened but he could only hear the waves slapping against the rock. As he watched, a hermit crab in the rock pool at his feet scuttled under the bladderwrack ...

This next writer has heightened the immediacy of the moment by using the present tense, and of the whole story by putting it into the first person — which also changes the feel of the tale, making it more human, less fantastic. Similarly, like many of the pieces, it moves away from the folk tradition (which is usually economic to the point of bareness) and towards a literary tradition (see *Had he been there before, he wondered?* in Example 10). The fact that these are all *written* versions makes this choice the more likely. A spoken retelling tends to make the teller use oral resources, including some or all the features of 'performance'.

Example 7

Waiting patiently, silently watching, holding onto the edge of the rock by my fingertips. I've only been here a few moments but my legs are aching and I've lost all feeling in my right toe. I daren't move in case I fall. The air is filled by the crashing and rolling of the waves. The spray constantly batters my face and the stench of salty air fills my nostrils. Hold your lips closed, I say to myself, don't swallow the water.

Example 8

A more explicitly unpleasant experience still.

Exhausted, cold and wet, Usheen shivered on the rock. The sun seemed distant and unfriendly, the rock harsh and evil. He heard but did not see the stag arrive. The lapping, shifting water, the gentle rhythm of hooves upon sand ...

Next comes Usheen's journey down to Tir-Nan-Ogue — "down, down"

Example 9

Down into into the crystal water went the stag with Usheen on his back, deeper and deeper. No longer did the sun penetrate the water, no longer could the waves be heard upon the shore. Green fronds swayed in the deep as the travellers rushed by. The strangest sea animals appeared out of rocks to observe Usheen and the stag, purple fishes with silver tails, orange and blue turtles. They were diving deep towards a bottomless pit ...

And on to the Land of the Ever Young itself 'where everything is good, a place of beauty, all the beauties of heaven are there'.

Example 10

As they reached the sea bed Usheen was aware of a strange watery light. He slipped off the stag's back, who disappeared from sight. Usheen felt strangely at ease. Here were beautiful people walking in seaweed-lined caves. Had he been here before, he wondered? He meandered through a maze of caves till he reached a huge cavern ...

Example 11

Tir-na-nog was a wondrous place. The grass was long and lush and green — greener than the emerald isle itself. The water that ran in the streams sparkled and sang in the sunshine that shone every day. The flowers that grew gave off the sweetest perfumes, sweeter than all the perfumed oils of Arabia. The birdsong was so beautiful that the people of Tir-na-nog would stop, just to listen, in peace and stillness, not talking.

I shall move on for the last examples, in this selection of enlargements of scenes from the story, right to the end where Usheen is at the ruins of his home, near the water trough which is to be his downfall. As you will see from the transcript of my telling, my account is somewhat embroidered, but not as richly as these:

Example 12

The water looked pure and cold, and as Usheen sat on his horse he watched the silvery droplets plink into the mossy trough, and watched them send ripples of iciness across the surface to the granite edges. Oh, what desire struck Usheen at that moment as he recollected days which had been full of bravado, companionship, love and earthiness! Usheen felt the warm body of the horse beneath his legs and watched its steamy breath as he relived those happy days...

Example 13

What a fool I have been. My very bones grow old, my eyes weak, my breath rattling in my chest. It was the water, the clear, sparkling splash of the water in the trough that fooled me. Me, with eyes as blue as the sea, to be so short-sighted, to be so misled, and now so old! Always water. It was the cold blue of the sea that day, so long ago now it seems, that chilled my thoughts as I swam to the rock out in the bay. The dark chill rock splashed by the waves where I waited for what I both dreaded and coveted.

That is a good note to move from expansion to actual additions — though as you will see by now, such a distinction is a fine one. Also observable is that there are marked shifts of ambiance when a reteller adds new texture to a given situation. The state of affairs for Usheen on the rock, for instance, is a good deal more uncomfortable than I imagined it.

2 The addition of new incident

As I read through the retellings I have accumulated I am aware of a continuum of additions ranging from bits of plumping out, as in Example 1 above, to additional entire episodes in an otherwise 'faithful' representation of the story, right through to transformations which produce stories distinctly different in tone and content. It is the middle range I shall illustrate next, from one author only.

This version is a particularly lengthy, fluent and easy read, an individual's 'revisioning' of the story as I told it but laced throughout with added rich detail. It shifts a gear, however, when Usheen returns to his old world. This portion is covered in one sentence of my telling: "And they put Usheen and his horse down in his own land and the warrior rode and rode until he came to the place where he was born."

This new version begins:

Usheen said goodbye, mounted the horse and rode off, his cloak flowing behind him. The Rulers watched him with sadness. The black horse ran like the wind and they rode through lands that Usheen had never seen. The horse needed no directions or guidance and travelled through through forests and rivers, over mountains and plains.

Usheen bends down to drink some five hundred words later; here are some of them:

Night was approaching but still the horse did not stop. Usheen saw in the distance a small cottage, smoke curling out of the chimney and a light shining in the window. As Usheen got nearer he could see an old woman standing by the cottage. She beckoned and pointed to the window. Usheen could see a blazing fire and a table set with food and drink. In a corner of the room was a bed, the coverlet thrown back. Usheen felt an almost overpowering weariness but he could still hear the warning. Even the wind in the trees seemed to be telling him not to get off the horse.

When he resists the invitation, the cottage, its occupant and everything in it disappear. Soon afterwards he begins to recognise features in the landscape that are familiar from his old days.

Excitement was growing as he approached his former home. Everything seemed the same, smoke slowly drifting up in the morning air. As he approached a man came out of the house and looked at the rider. The horse stopped and Usheen got ready to greet his brother. The man smiled but not with recognition and Usheen found himself staring into the face of a stranger.

Inevitably such additions underline or alter significant elements of a story. The situation at this point is certainly fantastic because of how Usheen came to be where he is, yet the Irish earth is real enough; it is also symbolic of all who, literally or metaphorically, try to get themselves back to their youthful past; and Usheen is, inevitably, totally alone in his venture. The additions made in this new version lift his whole quest into a nightmare Kafka-esque dimension, consequently it has a more unnerving effect on the reader. Here there are shades of the sinister side of looking longingly over one's shoulder to the past. Better, perhaps, to be a fully-fledged member of the here and now — which, if my version of *Usheen* is to be believed, may then be perceived as the land of the ever young!

3 Addition/substitution — familiar matters of today

Broadly speaking, there are two major elements to this story — the familiar and the magical. I like this kind of story best, though Usheen is not such a subtle intertwine of the two as is, for instance, *The Fisherman and the Mermaid* which seems to me to have implied within it a much more complex weave of both aspects, therefore it is open to a larger variety of retellings. Usually the addition of substantial amounts of direct speech effects a leaning towards the humanising of a fictional situation. One retelling which I have follows all the incidents of the story as revealed in my 'original' but a great deal of speech is added with the result I have just suggested; here is some of it:

"What a wonderful animal! Where did it go?" ...
"It's there and safe," yelled Usheen, "but how can I reach it?" ...
"Come away, it is late" "Yes, we must go home" ...
"Where have you been?" demanded their mother, concerned for the safety of her three young sons.

I must add, though, that while the story is the more 'domesticated' for the inclusion of normal, colloquial talk among the characters, occasionally speech has the reverse effect if it is presented in a heightened form — "Your serene majesty, I have prepared myself to perform your every bidding" kind of thing.

Emphasis on the family (Usheen interacting with his brothers comes first to mind in this context) can occur as relatively slight additions. However, such folk stories as this can step right out of the wonder tale tradition and into a more contemporary mode through certain kinds of substitution. My first three examples illustrate slight shifts towards an everyday atmosphere.

Example 1

Usheen was a fine, handsome lad, tall, blonde and broad-shouldered, in fact the apple of his mother's eye (my underlining).

Example 2

Usheen and his brothers talked at the supper table.

Example 3

But for several nights he had been dreaming of his brothers and the fun they had had — riding, hunting, exploring the countryside around their home. He longed to see them again and talk about old times over a glass of wine.

The third one here clearly adds to the idea of three young men enjoying earthly pleasures together. In the next example the young men have been made more boyish and the events are put chattily into the mouth of one of the brothers. Both the following writers have nudged the story even closer to a familiar world:

Example 4

I remember the summer before last when my two brothers and I were playing chase amongst the fields beyond the house. Sean was running down by the stream when he spotted a rather special stag — I say special because it was completely white ...

Several authors chose to invent a storyteller and a setting for the actual narration of the tale. Almost invariably this device anchors the story to reality. In this case it is couched in an oral world of childhood more strongly than the previous one:

Example 5

-Hey, look at that funny rock! It looks like melted wax gone hard. I wonder how it got out there in the middle of the lake? Can we swim out to it, Mum? Please, Mum?
-No you cannot! That's a very dangerous place.
-But Mum, it's only a rock!
-It may look like a rock but my grandfather told me when I was about your age that on that rock is the gateway to the Land of the Ever Young ...

Perhaps there are primary school teachers who instinctively want to take to the young stories about the young. One writer made a total substitution by producing a story about three boys who, while playing together, meet a stranger, an older boy, who eventually whisks one of them away to a land of "fun and adventure", reminiscent of the fate of the Pied Piper's children, where the boy enjoys himself until he begins to think it must be time to go home:

Example 6

They stopped searching for hidden treasure when he said, "Come with me and I'll show you a place where you can play forever." They followed him, struggling up the steep hillside and scrambled over a wall into the field beyond. As they ran along the edge of the field, avoiding the cow pats, the older boy ran ahead until he was out of sight. The youngsters stopped and scratched their heads. "That wasn't much fun" ...

O'sheen decided to scramble to the top of the hill to the far side of the field and lie in wait for the older boy, hiding behind a nearby barn ...

O'sheen heard their voices and when the older boy approached he pounced on to him. As they tussled they fell against the barn door, falling into the barn. There was the most wonderful world of fun and adventure any child could wish for.

Changing the age of the main character(s) in the story always has a pronounced effect. Even if the story remains a magical one, such a change does seem to make it more recognisably close to life and further from Peter Pan timelessness. In the next two examples, the hero becomes more real as the ritualistic significance of, first, old age and, second, youth which comes of age is attached to the situation. In each, Usheen is not simply a folk figure, 'one of the last of the Irish warriors', but someone who has reason to feel that life is especially sweet. Such moments are familiar to us all.

Example 7

Usheen had been a fine young man once. In his youth he had a full head of black hair and his eyes shone and sparkled. Though now grey haired, still a strong man having spent his life hunting in the forests around his home. When the physicians told him he had but days to live, he called his brothers all together around him.

"I would hunt again" he said, and next day he and his brothers went out into the forest together.

Example 8

Now on his eighteenth birthday O'Shanee's father presented him with a special gift — it was a bow — the finest one that O'Shanee had ever seen.

"Now that you are a man," said his father, "you shall have a man's bow." ...

At once O'Shanee knew that this bow was worthy of much greater things. He would search the forest until he found the King of the forest and the mountains, a stag of such proportions that it had become part of the legend of Perangue ...

At first they were surrounded by the sound of birdsong but as the sun rose higher the air became very heavy and gradually all sound ceased, save that of the crackling of snapping twigs and the occasional snort from the horses as they laboured upwards. The brothers said nothing but each one was acutely aware of the atmosphere of the occasion.

The sense that the story is occurring upon the real earth is further aided by that addition of a place name, Perangue. Localised specifics like this, including items associated with a particular cultural group and its way of life add further to the credibility of incredible happenings. Here are a few sentences out of a fine piece, the style of which is nicely not quite colloquially companionable, not quite traditionally distanced.

Example 9

Now the O'Shae brothers, I must tell you, hunted daily for rabbits along this rugged coastline. Until two days ago never had they seen any kind of deer, not to mind such a splendid creature as this. And yet they knew every crack and cranny of this part of Northern Kerry. Hadn't their mother sent them out with their father and uncle for rabbits almost as soon as they could sit in the saddle?

The brothers drew in their horses' reins and watched. Would the stag perform the same strange feat as it had on the previous occasions? Would it climb down from its lofty place and swim out into the sea toward the Blaskets and disappear from view just where the curragh carrying the young workers to Dingle sank twenty years ago with no survivors?

Now Sean's old mother still saw him as a day-dreamer, a romantic, in spite of his forty years. She had warned his younger brothers to make sure he didn't wander from the familiar track .

No place names in this next extract but it is steeped in the minutiae of a recognisable portion of England.

Example 10

On a grey day in the Northern hills clad in a dull patchwork of fields and lanes, a girl was born.

She was the first grandchild of Sarah, a dumpling of a woman, with her white hair in a bun. Midwifery held no secrets for Sarah who helped in all the village births and indeed in deaths. The baby was wrapped in a woollen blanket and placed in a drawer on the floor in her grandma's bedroom. The mother rested in the mahogany bed on the deep flock mattress. Downstairs in the living room the fireside boiler bubbled, heated by the coals which cracked and spat onto the clip rug, sending the striped cat running outside.

Sarah was already preparing the heavy wash tub and mangle for the bedding wash — the clothes line hung over the flat wall that ran the length of the street. "Monday's child is fair of face" — washday anyway in this household.

The remains of Sunday's ham with soaked peas plopped in the iron pan on the gas ring by the shop stone. Peeled potatoes waited ready in their pan on the hearth where the copper kettle proudly stood.

In the old armchair, covered in its multicoloured crochet shawl, lay the old flat cap — Frank's cap. His walking stick with its metal band now took on greater significance — he was a "grandad". Out mending the dry stone walls, he was unaware of the occasion. His sons and daughters at the mill would receive the news happily. This was a loving family and its extension into the next generation was to be welcomed.

Many seasons have passed in the street of mill cottages. The patchwork colours have changed in the fields, though the shapes have remained unaltered.

The flat wall in front of the row is a monument to the ten houses whose wives cleaned the flagstones with orange donkey stone on Fridays. Grass covered the area, looked down on by nettles sprung above submerged cellars.

Stories have been made and told. Some have been locked in the heart of that little November girl who wished to stay in her grandmother's house forever …

Whether that — unfinished — account was intended to be the setting of a new version of the Usheen events or, as in Example 5, the setting for a narration of it, I cannot say. It was certainly the most 'domestic' I have seen.

In the final extract here, the story is told very much in the present on a sunny picnic day by an old woman to her daughter whose children are splashing happily nearby in that very significant water trough ...

Example 11

The voice wraps comfortably around her as Gran begins to tell of the Long Ago when there was no steel, glass, concrete and tarmac landscapes, when flashing digits did not rule existence and people did not rule the earth. In that Long Ago time past, but here in this present spot lived a family of brothers — the O'Sheens — and a rip roaring lot they were by all accounts. The O'Sheen features were stamped on all of them and to have met them separately you would have known them to be from the same family. Five there were in all, each tall, and straight hair as black and wild as the bare branches that caught at it when they galloped, hunting through the winter woods, with eyes as blue as this afternoon's sky above you that laughed when they did — which was often for they loved life and one another.

Always together they were. Each would have died for the other ...

This long piece, also unfortunately unfinished at the time of the workshop, promised to be a beautiful blending of the palpable present and the infinite past. From the author's added notes it is clear that she intended the children at the picnic to be revealed as the descendents of the O'Sheen brothers. The whole tale was to tell that the family itself perpetuates Youth through its progeny and, metaphorically, through its own stored stories. A happy thought.

What intrigues me in all this is that listening to a tale such as Usheen stirs up in some people a strong consciousness of human experience as they have come to know it. It is therefore this which emerges and often dominates their own retellings (see Example 10 above): such retellers will often draw quite directly upon the accumulated evidence of their own lives, and those of members of their family, older and younger, including their knowledge of particular localities. All is called forth to give validity to an otherwise highly fictionalised set of characters and events. I have to add that when the retellers concerned are well known to me — my own pupils — I can anticipate who are most likely to do this; sometimes it is the ones who have most need to make sense of, or come to terms with, what they have lived through. Consciously or not, they will choose to do this safely and anonymously via a fictional story.

Thus it is that two in-built resources of such a reteller are activated here: the detail of the way he or she lives life and, secondly, the individual's own feelings and attitudes towards this personal experience. Leaving aside any therapeutic value to this, such components certainly make fine stories.

4 Addition/Substitution — matters of wonder and faerytale

If the previous group of writers have moved the story towards our own age, the next take theirs into a timeless sphere.

Example 1

This is a story, some might say a very strange story, of a land far away, a long time ago ...

The cards are on the table, and not for a game of Happy Families. The author's intent is to leave the home fires burning and venture into a realm of mystery and surmise.

Example 2

Long ago, back in the mists of time, it is said that there lived a hunter named O'Sheen, a fine figure of a man ...

Example 3

In the days of old, of mystery and magic, there lived a warrior named Usheen. Usheen would go hunting on his beautiful black horse, holding the rein with one hand and in the other would be his trusty spear.

Intertextualised by implication are all the magical tales of heroic deeds we have ever read or heard or invented for ourselves in the course of fleeing the muddle and banality of ordinary living. I must admit to being drawn to this kind of story metamorphosis when I look at a batch of retellings. It reminds me of my addiction to plainchant and the ethereal quality of a treble voice singing Byrd or Tallis: the more dehumanised the sound, the more I am soothed by the sense of an abstract order which exists beyond present mirth and tears. Pure escapism!

Here is a rather more dramatic starter:

Example 4

Silence lay over the forest like a blanket of snow, not a single breath of wind nor a glimmer of life. The earth lay dead.

Far away in the distance came a muffling, shuffling sound, leaves began to rustle, twigs began to snap as the rumbling crept nearer and nearer.

Suddenly like a zig zag of lightning a stark snow white stag flashed across a clearing like a thing possessed ...

This writer substituted the Usheen family for a family of white stags, more akin to unicorns than anything of the earth. It bears almost no resemblance to the original. Such pieces as I am quoting under the present heading move easily into a poetic mode, unlike those in the previous category which lean towards the speech and behaviour of ordinary people.

Example 5

They parted the laughing lips of the sea and dived deep into the dark waters. The beast thrust on deeper and Usheen followed through the darkness which pulled at his loose flowing hair, deeper and darker until the depth blossomed through its intensity and richness into golden light. Tir nan oge had found him, pulled him to herself through dark cold embrace to blissful and pulsating light. The beast he had so keenly pursued with his brothers for all its splendours was no longer to be seen — yet it was all around him.

Time slid into the future but Usheen was not aware of it. Age did not touch him. Suspended in splendour and light, no sound or sight marked him. Light itself surrounded him and his every moment was music ...

The water [of the trough] beckoned, reflecting the light and laughter of years, singing sweetly as a flute. Usheen leant and reached, but still so many years away and removed from his touch. The water teased and called. Usheen turned in his saddle as his leg swung over behind him and touched the ground.

It must already be clear that my motive in classifying these retellings under one heading is that the creative possibilities of this 'wondertale' approach, both imaginatively and linguistically, are quite breathtaking. The extracts which follow are taken from a retelling which makes this point better than I could. Here the tone of another time and place is sustained throughout even in passages of dialogue, and all its truth is metaphor.

Example 6

Oisin had hunted the great stag for all that day. He had hunted it all the day before. It had drawn Oisin and his brothers through brake and briar. It weaved through thicket and thorn as slick as a shuttle through the yarn, and whenever they were ready to give in, whenever its white scut only flickered between branch and bole, it would stop and let them come close and then be off again like a dream ...

Twice it rose out of the water, climbing without effort to the pinnacle of a great rock that reached up from the bed of the sea. And twice, beyond bowshot, beyond the range of the strongest arm, it had stood and stared into the very eyes and souls of Oisin and his brothers, and an amused and arrogant stare it was ...

Tonight I will stay here and tomorrow you, my brothers, will hunt the great stag again and drive it through the forest to this same place. I will swim to the rock and hide, and when the beast comes again to the rock I will take it and kill it ...

The darkness of the deep water filled Oisin's eyes and there was a roaring in his ears and he was afraid. Down they went and down until there was nowhere else to go and the stag let Oisin down.
And it was light.
Where is this place, said Oisin.
This is where time never passes, said the stag. This is where there is no growing old.

And the stag told him the name of the place. And vanished.
The people who lived there were young like Oisin and as beautiful as he was.
There was hunting and feasting, dancing and singing, and a hundred years of
living there was like half an hour in the land that Oisin had left …

The rulers of that place said: You are not wise, Oisin. No one can ever go back
to the same place. But the wish of your heart we cannot gainsay or refuse … If
your feet should touch the earth, all the years of that world will come on you.
Remember. Remember …

It was all changed terribly. The fields were rank. The streets were empty. The
roofs of the houses were fallen in and trees grew in the empty rooms. And his
own home, the home of his brothers, of his mother and sisters and the home of
his father had tumbled to a rubble of stones that were grey with lichen.

Oisin wept for all that was gone, and wept and wept for the ghosts that had
danced and sung and loved and fought in that house …

As his feet touched the earth the years of the world came upon him; his black
hair turned ash white, his cheeks fell away, his back bowed and he sank to the
ground under the weight of the years and the light died in his eyes, and Oisin
was dead and dust.

5 Substitution: the story as a trigger

This is perhaps the most intriguing transition of all. Suddenly, among
the recognisable versions, up comes one that bears little or no
resemblance to the original story. I have already mentioned a version
which was about stags, not people. Another version, though about
three brothers certainly, is actually all about the isolation of the
youngest, he being the weakest and the most dominated, and about his
final escape from misery. Together one day at the beach they see, on
the crest of a high breaking wave, a white stallion riding on the surf.
The vain efforts of the two older brothers to trap the animal are
described but it is the youngest brother who is allowed to make contact
and finally is spirited away on its back to a land where he is, at last,
strong, healthy and free from torment.

When a story is changed to this extent it is nearly always because the
author is occupied with one specific issue thrown up during the
storytelling, which may be embedded in the story itself or, as in this
case, may have been simply triggered by something comparatively

trivial — such as the fact that there are in Usheen three brothers with the spotlight on one of them; the listener may be intertextualising all those stories where the youngest sibling of three is the most disadvantaged in some way or other. Particularly independent-spirited people will compose totally new stories, and those with very strong views about, for instance, race or gender. Individuals who see themselves as rebels, especially among the young, may play the sceptic by producing a parody of the story in a very colloquial current idiom. Often these are very amusing.

Finally, a series of extracts from one retelling only. At first it fooled me. I thought, in spite of *brothers* being plural in Tir-nan-Oge, its opening sentences would lead into the events of my story, perhaps with a twist at the end which would allow them to be reunited in that desirable place:

Now Liam and his brothers lived in a place beyond this place. And you won't know about that place unless, like me, you have been woken from a dream and thought to yourself, "Oh, I've dreamt of a place where I would always want to be". And you've cursed yourself for waking, but no matter how much you've tried to remember that place you can only remember the way of things and what happened but not the most important thing: the way it feels to live in that place. For that place is called Tir-An-Noag and we all know of that place if we are human and if we can dream.

I should have suspected the arrival of a very different tale indeed. There is a clear change in the style of telling, with meta-narrative just under the surface. A short digression on this topic might be appropriate before this storyteller resumes.

Nothing is easier to underestimate than the resources which a teller brings to a story, for we are so finely tuned to the presence of these resources, have lived so long with them, have taken them in like the air around us that, like the complexities of everyday speech, they are naturalised for us. For teachers, however, it is worth giving a little consideration to some of these resources so that we appreciate more fully the non-simplicity of storying. Meta-narrative, for instance, which is a name for all those parts of a story, however slight, which refer to the story as such. Thus we find the familiar, "I first heard this story when ..." or "You're not going to believe this but ..." or even "To cut a long story short ...". Once we identify this ubiquitous enticement of the listener or reader, we do more than just appreciate it as a weapon in the armoury. We see its many different forms and subtleties. A well-developed story-telling project would engage a class or group in examining all this and observing which of the participants does this or that and what difference it makes.

The extracts below from this one retelling show one of the less obvious features of meta-narrative. Here the teller steps out of his story to talk to those receiving it. This is one of the many ways in which story writers go on borrowing from the oral tradition. "You" they say to us as though we are sitting around them, all readers of poetry with books on our shelves, as in the next extract. Notice, too, that this form of meta-narrative is a kind of meditation in which the narrator makes his or her presence felt, stepping out of the narrative to buttonhole us. It has its risks. An error of judgement and we'll be saying, "Get on with it! This is supposed to be a story not a sermon". Perhaps this is a good moment to see how my storyteller manages to walk this razor edge.

And in that place called Tir-An-Noag everyone is young. And half of those books on your shelves there would need no writing in Tir-An-Noag, for like me you read books of poetry and what is poetry but one half writing about My True Love and another half writing about Why Must My True Love Die? But in Tir-An-Noag true love lasts forever.

And in Tir-An-Noag there are no schools, for people know things in their hearts.

Now Liam and his brothers Declan and Sean lived in Tir-An-Noag. They lived in a lush green valley where everything was provided for them and they did not need to hunt or kill for they only needed to spill the fruits of the trees into their hands and they were fed.

For a tale which begins by describing a dreamlike paradise it seems also to have a lot of things to say, both on and between the lines, about the real world we are living in. This teller's meta-narrative is his channel for ideology and he walks his razor edge confidently. Many stories, such as *The Fisherman and the Mermaid*, seem more likely than *Usheen* to provoke highly innovative retellings which turn on some moral, social or political preoccupation on the part of the authors. Often these retellings have a far more persuasive strength than any formal argument making the same points.

In this retelling, the brothers' idyllic life is interrupted by the appearance of a stranger riding on a black stallion whose mission is to return to another place to meet with his brothers. Liam determines to join the stranger — called Usheen — in spite of his warnings:

You must not come with me for my land is not like your land and the people in my land have a terrible knowledge; nor can they do anything without wondering why they do it or what lives are for and all the people in my country would like to live here.

But Liam has discovered a terrible thirst for knowledge and, incidentally, a desire *to hunt wild beasts and kill living things.* Not long after he arrives upon the stranger's earth he hears

a drumming sound and it wasn't like the music Liam had heard in Tir-An-Noag. The music did not dance and meander so that you had to clap your hands and pick up your heels and grab each others hands and wheel your partners around to its beat. This drumming was staccato and insistent and repetitive ...

... he saw men all wearing the same clothes: dark helmets with holes cut for them to see. And Liam ran towards the men, thinking they must be hunters. Usheen leapt from his horse and ran to stop him.

The men with balaclavas raised their guns and pointed them past Liam towards Usheen. For they recognised him. Wasn't this the man their enemies spoke of? Wasn't this Usheen whose spirit would live forever? Didn't his name live on in the legends of their enemies?

And they fired.

We are not told the fate of the fictional Liam. Whatever it might have been is of little consequence compared with the fate of an oppressed Irish nation. That, without a doubt, played no part in my rendering of the *Usheen* story which triggered this one.

Chapter 3
NATE: GAINING CONFIDENCE
with *Little Jack* by Lynda Jones

First comes the anticipation, the nervous tension.

This was certainly so for me. It must also have been so for the course members of the Commission I had agreed to run at the NATE Conference, 1990, titled *Storytelling in the Classroom*. "This commission," I had written months before for the Conference handbook, "will focus upon the creative potential of teachers as storytellers. The aim will be to convince each participant that he or she IS a storyteller who will go back to the classroom keen to give storytelling a major place in the curriculum. Stories will be shared ..."

We would all be 'performers', some willingly, some not so willingly.

This was to be my most major in-service assignment ever. It involved a series of practical sessions — workshops. As this is the biggest meeting of English language specialists from primary, secondary and higher education in the country, I had some qualms, to say the least, in agreeing to such a task. It would mean working with twenty or more teachers — who would have high expectations — over a period of days: not my usual here-today-but-gone-tomorrow encounters. On the other hand, it could be pleasurable to get to know these people and participate in a more ongoing creative enterprise than time normally allowed, all to the cause of improving the quality of the classroom.

There might well be some who would be newcomers to the NATE conference, and/or to storytelling, and new, perhaps, even to the teaching profession. I would have the chance to watch their confidence growing within the situation, and mine along with them. But what if some real experts turned up ...?

In the event there were both 'extremes' in my group — the complete beginners (as they chose to see themselves) and at least one person whom I would describe as a sophisticate in the field of storytelling in the classroom. On the surface, at least, each situation was very different from the other. I suspect, however, that what divided them at the beginning of that conference was just the length of time each had spent on the same road which leads to total commitment to the centrality of storytelling in the curriculum. Both, of course, were storytellers but only one was able to acknowledge the fact.

By the time I got down to planning the work of my commission, my affections had settled around *The Fisherman and the Mermaid* (see Part 3, page 174). I felt it was ideal for a focus of the activities I had in mind. I intended that these should involve the participants directly in most, if not all, of the kinds of work which my pupils had done in my primary and secondary classrooms over the years. Ideal or not, the fact was that this story was my big favourite of the moment, reason enough to put it at the centre of the course, or, to be literal, at the beginning of it.

Its impact is much reduced here for the reader compared with that of the listener, yet the tale is rich enough to win attention even in print: you'll see why I like it so much. I knew in my bones that it would go down well at NATE. It never fails with children of any age, but an adult audience, knowing from experience about love and parenting, and all else that maturity brings, can benefit from a whole added dimension of perceptions while listening to the story.

In advance of the conference I received a list of the names of the members of my commission. There were two categories of teachers among the twenty-one in my group: those I had met before (two) and the unknowns, just names on a sheet of paper (nineteen). Of the two, there, to my joy, was George Murphy, famous in my memory for *Grass* (see page 62) though his face had become a blur. It was great to have an enthusiast whom I had met once and liked a lot. The other was Jean Dunning, familiar both as a friend and a fellow founder-member of our London Narrative Group of teachers interested in storytelling in the classroom. But ... though I was sure she had not heard me tell this particular story, she had been witness from the start of my 'going public' in the world of storytelling: would I be likely to have something to offer her that she had not heard before? She herself was an accomplished teacher/storyteller and, much worse from my point of view, was that she was in the final stage of completing a doctorate thesis on storytelling. A PhD person: suddenly she sounded different from the friend I knew her to be. What could *I* offer her?

And what if people should refuse to do the tasks I set them?

I am the purveyor of the story. The story is the key, the key to each listener's store of creative potential, come who may! It is always so, I told myself busily. Anyway, storying must be much more fun than thesis-ese and it will be nice for me to be able to count on at least one encouraging face to boost my spirits. Thus I battled with my own nerves while, no doubt, somewhere else in the land, prospective members of my group were battling with theirs.

Known or unknown, these teachers would, I felt sure, be drawn into this old tale. I pondered over their possible responses to the fisherman story. It has the sadness of the fisherman who begins with loneliness and returns to it, of the children left motherless and the mother left childless. It has the joy of the mermaid's ecstatic return to her own element, and the fisherman's respite from his solitary life — better to have loved and lost, etc; and even after his wife has gone back to the sea he still has his children's company. Any feminists present will approve the mermaid's successful return to her chosen situation or, if they take themselves especially seriously, will see the tale as a piece of shameful abduction and start a good argument or two.

Will they lean towards the make-believe or the village reality? The lyricisms or the domesticities? Will some prefer the self-sufficiency of solitude to the dependence of companionship ... or would they see things the other way round?

What visual images will people conjure out of the scenes of the story? Will the items selected be enveloped in moonlight or sunshine, shadow or the glow of a peat-fired hearth? What voice will they give to the mermaid? A 10-year-old Asian girl, working with a group of pupils who were taping their own version of this story in a primary classroom I had visited not long before, had sung in Malayalam — a language from the south of India — and had intoned the mermaid's every speech in the same language, the child's own mother-tongue. This had added a new aura of mysticism to the identity of the mermaid. Maybe some course members would involve their own native languages and dialects.

And would this new set of listeners have their feet so firmly on earth that they would be unwilling to enter the mermaid's watery world and speculate within her preferred element? I had plans to get them writing poetry just as we might expect our own pupils to do. I had up my sleeve a beautiful poem by Seamus Heaney, whose version of the story had inspired me to mine, which dwelt upon the mermaid's 'first sleep' on her return to the sea and her shedding of earthly taints. I wanted them to see it after they had tried something similar

101

themselves, while too flushed by the pleasure of composition to feel put down by a master of the art!

I began to look forward to my next assignment.

Of course there might be some who would be reluctant to meet the freedom offered by composing a poem or retelling a story. Freedom craves confidence.

Suddenly it was all happening. The group convened and people introduced themselves — a helpful procedure for me though, I gathered later, unnerving for some. There were those who would prove uneasy sharers of their skills: "I've never told stories, except to my own children [*what a pleasant vision that conjures up, I think to myself*], I've come here to learn." I know the feeling. If I had a penny for all the occasions when I have myself been in a group large enough to allow me to preserve unobtrusively my own silence I would be well off. My task would be to eliminate such reticence by providing not only the stimulus of the story itself but, somehow, the incentive to make people bold.

For a fleeting moment I wished wearily that I were back at home doing the crossword with my husband, beside me a mug of tea and Flotsa, my cat. Why do I accept these invitations?

Then I launched into *The Fisherman and the Mermaid*.

At the end of that first session I asked the course members to prepare a retelling of *The Fisherman and the Mermaid* by the next day, to be 'performed in small groups' — groups of three, in fact. As one person had not yet arrived at the conference the numbers did not quite divide by three so I joined the leftover group, a pair, in fact. It was George, and the woman who, at the opening session, I remembered, had firmly stated that she had come to learn and was "very weak on story *telling*". She was Lynda. I smiled at them and thought of *Grass*, the hilarious tale George had told in that Calderdale workshop — nearly two years ago, was it? — first in a small group and then, after unusually heavy pressure from me, to the whole group of about thirty teachers. I discovered from what he said when I joined the pair of them that morning that his confidence in telling stories had virtually begun with that particular Halifax storytelling. I hadn't bargained on the effect my reference to that occasion would have on Lynda. She presumed an expertise in George which was way beyond her own. And there she was, stuck in a group consisting of herself, George and the course leader. Here is a transcript of the talk which began our group encounter; it makes me cringe even now over my insensitivity to Lynda's state of mind:

Me *OK, who's going to start?*

They had all been told what to do. It did not even enter my head that anyone would back off — though I expected there would be some who would not manage an entire story. After all, the evening after our first session had been crammed with activity and most people at such conferences, when all's done, make for the bar — rather than the 'study' or the narrow hall-of-residence bed which I, as a tired fusty-crusty, settled into gratefully.

L. *Not me.*

[Laughter. Hers somewhat tremulous.]

L. *I feel in a formidable group here. I've already said that I feel very much ...* [next words inaudible on tape]

Me *Really? Why? Let's put this off.*

I smell trouble and put off the tape recorder, having already explained that it was present only because I had learned my lesson from not having had it in on the go when I had first heard George's story of the twinnies.

Whatever it was that Lynda then said by way of explanation for her enormous reluctance to tell a story I have now forgotten. What I remember with sickening clarity was the realisation that she was close to tears during the course of it. I quickly shifted our chat to George, who talked about *The Fisherman and the Mermaid* and how it had affected him. I was hoping that if she heard a version of the story from him which (inevitably) would be totally different from what she had thought up, Lynda would find the confidence to have a go.

After a while, she began to join in with the conversation with an occasional monosyllable, and I felt brave enough to put the tape recorder back on, though I certainly did not expect to get more than just George's retelling: I like to think I would never force anyone to tell a story against their will!

G. *Ay, colours. The colours of the daylight, daylight and that rural world. And that contrasted with twilight and the colours of the moon and the sea ...*

Now if I were to try to retell the story there would be certain props for me that I would have to have to hang my story from ...
the moonlight was quite a potent force ...

I see the mermaid going back to the shore ...

[George was talking at some length, almost to himself.]

Me *This is what mattered to George, as it were, or one of the things. This is what people do, you'll have some people, for instance, be angry with the fisherman, they'll take a feminist view ...*

[more chat, mainly between me and George while out of the corner of my eye throughout, I was watching for the return of Lynda's composure.]

Me *... Well, are you going to have a try then, George?*

Long pause.

G. *Um, a part of the story which —*

[so George is still avoiding the telling, is still just talking about it! Maybe he's nervous, too.]

— What I found very affecting was the part where the fisherman goes down to the shore, sees the mermaid sitting on the rocks, her long black hair, and the sea rolling in, the noises of the waves and the shingle, the mermaid in her own world, the sense of the onlooker almost feeling guilty about being there but then guiltily noticing the cloak —

[who, I am wondering, is George now? the creator of the scene as onlooker? one who is recollecting his own listening to my story as an invited observer? or is he simply (simply?) identifying with the fisherman? Probably the latter.]

— next to him, and the legend of the cloak ...

etc. At the finish he talks about another story he had heard me tell when he had a completely different reaction. I begin to worry about Lynda's marginalisation

G. *... with this one, I think there is a poetic quality in it I would want to catch...*

[He finally says he wants to work on it and I, at that point, am wondering what I am missing from what is going on in the other groups where people are patently being storytellers!]

Me *So you'd want to work on it. Yes. I sometimes do that if ... However, he's still avoided the issue! You see,* [to Lynda] *you're not the only one!* [We all laugh companionably.]

Me *"There she was, sitting on the rock, before his very eyes..." might be a way to start. Well, not your way, a way to start.*

L. *You see, I feel I need to make the story my own —*

[I am all ears.]

L. *— by changing the perspective of it —*

Me *Right!*

L. *—so I could tell it in the same way —*

Me *Yes, yes?*

L. *— so when I thought about telling it I wanted to choose, um, a different way of telling it, a different perspective. I suppose for me the moral issues that were raised were the most interesting aspects of the story. I wanted to be able to make, well, raise, the moral questions, not necessarily answer them but ask the questions explicitly which were implicit in the story so the approach I would adopt might let me do that. And I also wanted, I think, to bring the children more into it because for me — and I'm sure this is a very personal thing because I have left my children for the very first time ever to come here — the idea of the mermaid going back and stealing looks at her children, that is tears-to-the-eyes stuff whereas the fisherman's loneliness just didn't grab my attention. So, I suppose it's a personal thing —*

[Isn't it always, I think to myself! Isn't that the very miracle of retelling

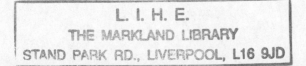

stories? Simultaneously, involuntarily, I recreate the stabbing ache of being away from my own children occasionally when they were very little a long time ago.]

L. — *which depends very much on the local circumstances* —

G. *On gender as well.*

L. — *and having* [word inaudible] *for children.*

I talk a bit about how I like telling stories which have a variety of layers and strands so there is something for everyone.

L. *And they'll take what they want from it.*

Me ... *so it can become a very, very different kind of story. You know you really haven't had a lot of time between yesterday and today to get a story prepared* —

[offered consolingly in preparation for an ignominious escape to some other group where teacher's 'unreasonable' demands have been met!]

Me — *I don't really know how people have managed, to be honest.* [To Lynda] *But if you were to go away and think about it and then meet George, say, in a month's time, you know* — *maybe if you did a written version, you know, that can be very satisfying, you know, a written version, when you've all the time in the world to reflect* — *you would find you each had very very different beginnings.*

Did you even get as far as trying to think of a possible opening for your story -

[enter, surreptitiously, my last-ditch attempt to salvage something in the face of my first ever 'failure' to get even a touch of a retelling in such workshop circumstances]

Me — *if you were to tell it?*

L. *Yes, I think so. Yes. Written out. Yes.*

Me *Would you fancy trying to tell just the start, or maybe read out what you've written?*

[To my amazement Lynda pulled out from papers on her knee what looked like a very long piece of writing! I could hardly believe my eyes. Who would have guessed?}

Me *Do you want to read it? Or would like to try and tell it, what you've written?*

[not a chance! But I don't want Lynda to think that I don't believe it's an option for her ...]

L. *I think I'd rather try and tell it.*

[... did I hear aright?]

Me *OK. We won't stare at you.*

L. *If I just ...*

Me *That's right. You have a little look through. Just take your time.*

[George and I have a separate quiet chat about how he would enjoy looking at the Seamus Heaney version of the story ... Lynda looks up.]

Me *Ready? Just start when you're ready. Maybe as you'd tell it to your own child.*

And start she did. A story which was from a point of view which I had not encountered before — that of the Fisherman's neighbours. A story which grew in richness as her storyteller's confidence took over. But then, she is a born storyteller. Like the rest of us. She simply she had not acknowledged herself as such. Most of us don't.

Lynda has one advantage which it would be wrong not to mention here: she has a lovely sounding voice which is soothing on the ear without drawing attention to itself. There are not many voices like that. It's almost like having nice music on Radio Three when I am concentrating on something else: my mind is active with other meanings while being comfortably disposed because of the music filling the air. I listened to her meanings while subconsciously being soothed by the texture of the sounds she made. I don't know many voices like that — unobtrusively easy voices. She's a lucky storyteller — the ideal voice for the role. There is someone on Radio Three called Susan Sharpe who has such a voice — one of the few voices I will listen to willingly on that station — "Get on with the music and cut the cackle" I usually say, often out loud. Speech irritates me on the music programme, especially on Saturday mornings and — frantically, hysterically — during the cricket season which erases the music altogether from my FM-less car radio ...

Lynda had such a mellifluous voice, which seemed to come into its own the moment she began to tell us her story. Here on the page are her words, without the soft sound of her speaking them — a sound which totally captured George and me in a way that none of our conversation had done up to that point. Everything else within and without the room in which we sat suddenly ceased to be.

L. *I suppose Jack's been around for really as long as I can remember. Even when I was a young girl he was a grown man. But he was isolated, friendless, didn't ever invite us to make friends with him and so we accepted that he wanted to be left alone. Sure, we would watch him as he went down to the shore, paced, looking out to sea, but days went by, months, I suppose years went by when he didn't really enter into our conscious life at all.*

Obviously we were all very surprised when he arrived with a wife, moreover a wife whose beauty surpassed the beauty of all the other women we'd seen. Sure, we were curious but he gave us no clues about where she had come from. As we became more aware of her in our life she still remained enigmatic with her long hair, and a smile that played around her lips. But her eyes were always distant, staring somewhere that we just couldn't fathom.

The years passed and she bore him two children, two girls first who grew straight, her hair and her smile. And then a little boy, very, very different, with his warmth and his arms that reached for you to hold him.

When, one day, she disappeared as mysteriously as she had come, we were just as surprised and at first there seemed no explanation for her disappearance.

Jack became withdrawn, quiet, just as he used to be and his young son whom they'd named Jack too, increasingly sought solace with us and would come and sleep with us in the room in the loft.

Three months later the girls went too [inaudible few words on tape] *though no one was really sure about that.*

I suppose we should have guessed that it was something to do with the relentless sea that governed their behaviour and their mother's. But when little Jack revealed to us one day what he had seen I think it was then that we began to piece together the mystery of the missing woman.

First he told us of a garment, a piece of cloth, that seemed to have come from a distant land, which fell from the roof when it was being mended, and how he had observed his father hide it away, secrete it away. He had told this to his mother in all innocence, it seemed, but it was from that day that she disappeared. We in the village began to recall the old days of mermaids who had left the sea and been kept captive by the men who had retained their garments.

That would have seemed to be the end of the story but for little Jack's tales of whisperings during the night and whenever he told us of these, there on the stair the next day were the salty remains of water that seemed to suggest the passage of someone who had been to visit.

Me I thought she said she couldn't tell stories. Didn't she say she couldn't tell stories, George?

In this restrained, economical retelling, she had indeed brought the children — one of them, certainly — 'more into it' and adopted a stance — the neighbours' viewpoint — which would allow her to 'make explicit the moral issues', thus using narrative directly as argument should she wish to re-work the story at some point in the future. But at that time what mattered, I need hardly add, was that she had held her audience completely spellbound. Even her pauses here and there, no doubt mere hesitancy, caused us to wait with even greater eagerness for the next bit of the story. And all from one who had set out, almost tearfully, to escape the ordeal of telling a story.

There were many excellent stories told that day and the poems which appeared at my request anonymously on the wall of our commission room were all very readable.

The Mermaid's Return to the Water

!

!

!

!

Long time
No Sea

There was no shortage of humour in the group, I'm happy to report!
Here is another:

Stateless

I suppose I should be grateful
at this necessary severance:
the sharp surface's cold blade of division.

I plunge into myself;
this is, after all, my body's element.

But see — love spreads itself away
in circles from my centre.
And I below in cold suspension.

One of the course members, John Davey, had said at the beginning of
the week that he'd joined the group because he was fed up with the
National Curriculum and thought this commission sounded like fun.
He didn't have a lot to say in the 'plenary' stints but had a twinkle in
his eye and a shrewd look about him. I couldn't resist testing my bit of
guesswork: "John, you see those two poems. I reckon you wrote one of
them."

"I wrote them both," said he.

Like (unlike?) the mermaid, perhaps, he's got the best of both worlds!

As for Jean Dunning, it was good to have her in the company and, of
course, she was a valued member of the group, one of the few who
volunteered to share her story with all of us (see Part 3, page 180). The
written version of her story arrived in the post some weeks later. On
the phone she told me she was writing up the experience of producing
it with a view to using the account in some suitably adapted form in
her doctorate thesis. When, at my request, she later sent it for us to see,
one reading was enough for me to realise its appropriateness here, as
an inspiration to all aspiring storytellers in the teaching profession and
beyond.

What she does not include is something she said to me towards the
end of the conference. She had told me that during a recent visit to

Paris she had seen a sculpture by Rodin, a carved head at the top of a huge piece of rough rock. As she looked at it she had thought, had Rodin wanted, he could have made anything, anything he wished, out of all that rock. "That is how I feel now about composing stories. There is an infinity of possibilities for me."

I was reminded of the words of a young mother who had become totally involved in composing and telling stories, mainly autobiographical about her family, as a result of attending a series of workshops for parents of primary school children run by Mary Medlicott in the London Borough of Redbridge. I had heard her on a television programme *By Word of Mouth* in January 1990 on Channel 4. She said that when her stories emerged it was as if they were coming out of a tiny hole in a huge balloon, full of stories she could tell if only there were time enough. It is like that for all of us. We must make as much of our good fortune as we possibly can.

Now, at the risk of some repetition, the whole experience of that NATE occasion is about to be relived by someone on the receiving end of it. But before I temporarily hand my story over to Jean Dunning there is one critical point I must make. Part 2 of this book makes minutely explicit the nature of my workshops. My hope is that I have talked myself out of a job — made myself, professionally speaking, redundant as a teacher/storyteller. All that is required is for one person (in a primary school, an English department or at an in-service gathering) who is hooked on telling stories to offer to tell a favourite story to colleagues. The story can then be retold in some way — prose, poetry, the beginning, the ending, a part of it or the whole — and the results shared. Such workshops do not need to incorporate the services of a Betty Rosen. The success of *Shapers and Polishers* is, as far as I am concerned, in direct proportion to the extent to which my readers will DO for themselves!

Chapter 4
NATE: A PARTICIPANT'S VIEWPOINT
By Jean Dunning

I have chosen to write the story of what was for me an unusual and important personal experience. It began at the annual conference of NATE at Manchester University (April, 1990) where I was one of a group of teachers and others involved in education, who explored oral storytelling as a means of teaching and learning with Betty Rosen, a teacher/storyteller. Our material was rich and diverse, including traditional tales, tales of personal experience and poems. Over the four days we worked together, Betty asked us to assume a variety of roles: the role of performer (the teller of the tale to small and large groups), the role of listener (within small and large audiences), the role of respondent (in thought and talk), the role of writer (writing a poem; preparing a retelling of the story).

These roles and consequent activities could be expected of students in any classroom where the telling and retelling of stories was the chosen mode of operating. I want here to follow one strand of the work we did from the point of view of the apprentice. I begin in the role of listener.

1 Listening to *The Fisherman and the Mermaid*

At the end of the first session. Betty told an Irish folk tale: *The Fisherman and the Mermaid*. She said that she was keeping quite close to the lyrical version composed by Seamus Heaney. Here is a prosaic summary of it.

A lonely fisherman lives in a cottage on the west coast of Ireland. One day he finds a mermaid sitting on a rock with her back to him, combing her hair with a comb of mother of pearl. Beside her on the rock is her magic garment.

He knows that without this garment she cannot return to the sea, so he steals it. The mermaid then follows him back to the cottage where she warms herself by the fire. Secretly, the fisherman hides the garment in the thatch of the roof. The mermaid becomes the fisherman's wife, they have three children: two girls and a boy, and live together, apparently happily, for some years. The fisherman forgets all about the magic garment but the mermaid does not. One day, the thatcher is repairing the roof of the cottage and comes across it, and leaves it lying among the straw. The mermaid's little son sees it and tells his mother. That night, the mermaid puts on her garment and returns to the sea, never to be seen again for sure.

"Now, I'm going to tell you a story." As Betty said this, discussion tailed off; we fell silent, expectant.

Assuming a soft Irish accent, she began. Her voice was confiding, inviting, sometimes almost singing, but never loud. The language she used was poetic: the magic garment, she said, "Was as blue as the blue of the sea, as green as the green of the seaweed, as brown as the sand of the shore and it gleamed in his hand like a fish." This language, like her voice, drew us away from the mundane world around us, into the special world of the story.

Paradoxically, as she distanced us mentally from our surroundings, Betty drew us closer into the circle by maintaining eye contact with us and by using restrained gestures and body language, appropriate to the small space between us. The interaction was both like and unlike intimate conversation and we were held by it, spellbound in the traditional way.

Betty sketched in the landscape setting of the story — the low white walled cottage with its thatched roof, beside the sea. She did not describe the timeless figures of the solitary fisherman and the beautiful mermaid in any detail, nor share their thoughts and motives with us. I was surprised, then, by the portrayal of the mermaid's young son. He was pictured, as he watched the thatcher at work, pondering what he would be when he grew up: a thatcher or a fisherman like his father? He was also pictured after his bath by the fire, being wrapped in a towel and hugged by his mother, then telling her the whereabouts of the magic sea-garment. The ending of the story was very vivid — the mermaid put on her magic garment and "leapt" into the sea. We were quietly withdrawn from the story-world by Betty speaking of the small wet footprints that were *said* to have been seen, leading to the children's bedrooms, as though the mermaid came to look at them at night. "But I don't know if this is true", said Betty, looking at the floor and so signalling that the telling was finished.

There was silence again for a few seconds, then movements, shuffles and sighs as we came back into the present.

2 Responding to the Story

There was an inner response going on in our heads throughout the telling and then the talking afterwards.

The Bond with the Teller

I have already indicated the performance artistry which Betty employed to entice her audience into listening and continuing to listen. Voice, language and gesture were all carefully attuned to establish and maintain her authority as storyteller. We all knew well enough the conventions governing our behaviour at such a performance, so we consented happily to listen without interrupting and became spellbound.

Beyond this, I felt that she was also using the texture of her narrative to enmesh us. Walter Benjamin in *Illuminations* writes of how storytellers, in retelling a traditional tale will leave their own 'fingerprints' upon it. These traces may be signs of their adapting the tale they have received to suit their present audience. When Betty depicted the domestic episodes about the mermaid's son, using naturalistic, concretely detailed description of thought and dialogue and miming the way the mermaid wrapped her son in the towel, she was doing just this. She knew that this audience was certainly interested in how children think about their own futures and how they are likely to confide in their mothers. (Several of us were also parents, some with young children.) Through these passages, Betty as a parent and teacher herself, was contacting us directly and personally and I sensed a smiling response from the audience to them.

It is also worth noting that, differentiating the son from the other characters by the way he was described and the amount of attention that was given to him in the story, drew our attention to the fact that he was crucial to the plot of the story and to the creation of suspense.

The Dialogue with the Text

Along with Betty's storyteller's magic, and not separable from it, the story itself, as an artistic creation, worked upon us; it was proved to be a good choice for us because we would not have gone on listening to it, however well it told, if it had seemed pointless. What, then, was in it for us? What processes were we going through in our minds as we listened so quietly?

Betty had freed us temporarily from the demands of the world around us enabling us instead to take up the spectator role. In this role, I think that what was happening in my own mind was something like the following:

I was visualising the story happening;
I was interpreting the story by referring it both to my own inner feelings and to my conception of the world outside myself;
I was evaluating the story and the telling of it;
I was thinking (more dimly) about the retelling I knew I was going to be asked to do later.

I believe that all these processes were happening simultaneously but, at one moment in the storytelling, one strand would be foregrounded and at another, a different one.

I may succeed in partly demonstrating the process with two moments I remember very vividly. As soon as Betty mentioned her, I could visualise the mermaid — not because she was described, beyond being beautiful and combing her long black hair — but because I already knew, culturally, about mermaids. I was unsure, though, about her 'magic garment'. What shape of garment was it? A dress? A scaly fish tail? How would she put it on? I could not *see* it. Then, Betty said that, as the years passed, so the fisherman forgot about the garment he hidden in the thatch, but, after a pause, "the mermaid did *not* forget". This antithesis and the emphasis on "not" helped me to put aside literal considerations. I saw that the mermaid could be any woman living with a secret sense of loss all her life. (Later, a member of the group used a scarf as the magic emblem in her version of the story.)

At the end of the tale, Betty used the word "leapt" to describe how the mermaid went back into the sea and, I recall, I felt this was the perfect choice because we speak of salmon leaping as well as people; therefore it was just right for a double-natured creature. By the end of the story, I was preoccupied with the mermaid's relief at re-entering her own element. I think we can see, in these instances, the movement from a piecemeal to a holistic response to the story which then takes place at a metaphorical level.

Any person who listens to a story must be involved in a critical evaluation of it as it is told, even if they are only expecting to be entertained: is this a good story? Could I tell it to my friends at work? How would it go down? This kind of thinking is the evaluating aspect of the inner dialoguing I have suggested. In our case, an audience who had come to hear a story with educational purposes in mind, wanting to learn how to tell stories or how to do it better, ourselves, and how to perform in the classroom, the critical edge was sharpened. No doubt other people were thinking, as I was, of particular classes with which they would have liked to try out the story, wondering how to retell it, what kind of accent it would be possible to use, and so forth. I enjoyed Betty's performance immensely and felt that I could not possibly match it — maintaining an Irish accent would be a problem for a start — but that I might have a go at telling my own version, whatever that turned out to be.

Voiced response

Immediately after Betty finished telling the story, two other women members of the group interrupted my train of thought.

One said, "Did you see that programme on TV about women who have left their children?" I had seen it and, although it had not been on my mind during the telling of the story, I saw that the association was highly relevant. It was a documentary in which a range of modern women's troubles were featured: the battered wife, the bored woman who described herself as "a prisoner in a rather beautiful prison", a young woman who had never had a chance to pursue her education and a woman unable to cope with the messiness of young children. All of these had suffered such pressure that they had sought peace and fulfilment by leaving their families. The mermaid was a metaphor for all of them. The second woman said, referring to the mermaid, "Of course, she was trapped, wasn't she?" For her, *that* was the important point of the story. When she said it, I saw it was true but it had not been the point I had concentrated on. Each of us chose the aspect of the story which fitted into our own internal landscape. Talking about our associations and comparing and exchanging our interpretations enabled our landscapes to overlap and so to enrich our individual perceptions of the story. The variety of our responses indicates the complexity of what might at first be thought to be a simple tale.

3 Writing

The Poem

Next, Betty read with us a poem that a class of 10-year-olds had composed after hearing *The Fisherman and the Mermaid*. Our attention was caught by the colour and light of the world they depicted. We read some other short poems and extracts of poems about the sea and then Betty asked us to write for the next morning a few lines about he first few moments after the mermaid re-entered the sea. We talked a little about imagery and someone said how the imagery of the story had been polarised into light and warmth for the world of the cottage and cold and darkness for the world of the sea. I felt that since this opposition suggested accepting the land dweller's world as preferable to that of the sea dweller and I wanted to adopt the view of the mermaid in my poem, I needed different imagery. I decided to oppose the hard resistance of land to the liquid supportiveness of the sea. This is part of what resulted:

I have so longed
To leave the dry harshness of the unmoving rocks,
To drop the pain of balancing on two feet,
To lose all heaviness
And slip, effortless, into my own
Endlessly welcoming element …

The poem ends with the mermaid trying, in giving herself back to the sea, to "Drown the sorrow of my children's pain".

There was an excitement about writing this which came out of the intensity of the whole morning's activity and was not unrelated to the wish to have something to contribute to the next morning's session. I think it is possible to detect how the talk after the story, as well as the other poems we read, had fed into what I produced.

Notes for a Retelling

The second task Betty gave us was to prepare for the next session our own new version of the story to tell to the group. She asked us to choose any new perspective on the story that appealed to us and to try to situate it in a place which had personal meaning for us.

My process of composition was as follows:

(a) I took up an idea suggested by one of the men in the group: that it would be interesting to think about the fisherman after the loss of his wife. Many ideas suggested themselves:

He saw her leaving and tried to stop her ...
He did not see her leave, but searched for her in the sea and drowned.
He was tortured with guilt for having trapped her in the first place.
What did he tell the children? That she had left with the thatcher? ...

It was hard to decide; there seemed to be so many possibilities.

(b) The second requirement, to set the story in a familiar place, made me think of using my Scottish roots. It was just possible I might be able to tell my story in a Scottish accent. But the place I had my strongest early connections with was inner suburban Manchester. What a contrast to the idyllic setting of Betty's story! This thought set me remembering how I used to long for the sea side in the summer when it was hot and dusty and how exciting it was, on the few occasions we did go to the sea, to be the first to glimpse it from the train.

(c) I invented a child, who has some connection with myself at the age of 6 or 7. She was to be the fisherman's granddaughter, child of the mermaid's son. I became intrigued by the possibility of affinities between the generations. The child must be somehow like the mermaid but live in an industrial city, longing for the sea. She would visit her grandfather and he would tell her his story. So, my central narrative structure was established: there would be the fisherman's story of the mermaid's disappearance framed within the story of his granddaughter's summer holiday.

(d) I began then to focus upon the mermaid's son, growing up motherless. I thought of him questioning his father, hearing rumours in the village, hints of scandal at school. What story about it all would he be able to live with? The question of the literal/sceptical turn of mind adopted by some young teenage boys, which makes them reject fantasy stories as childish, had been raised in one of our discussions. It was a phenomenon I had come across myself and I decided that the mermaid's son might have adopted this attitude as a form of self-defence when young. When questioned by his own child about the magic garment in the thatch, he would say, "It was only an old petticoat stuffed in a hole that the rats had made, to keep the wind out."

(e) Rapidly, I began to make notes. At this stage, I seemed to have done the important thinking about my version. It was as if, now, I had only to bring it out; I knew it was there, waiting to be given shape in words. The fisherman/grandfather told his story in the spare metaphorical way that Betty had told her version. It was important that his grandchild hear and believe him. Then she was given a kindly common sense version by her father. Who was she to believe? I felt it was important to leave the child to face the two explanations and to show that she was more drawn to the metaphorical by having her, at the end of the story, think she sees the mermaid standing in the shallows, looking towards the cottage with, perhaps, tears in her eyes. To have ambiguity at the end was very important, I felt.

(f) My version had become more complex than I had intended and just working it out had taken all my time. There was not time to practise telling it or to try out the Scots accent.

4 Retelling the Story

Next day, there were opportunities to tell our versions in both small and large groups. There was a good deal of reticence among the group at first about taking on the whole group audience, and in one or two cases extreme anxiety which was not conquered before the end of the conference. One person, who was already an accomplished teller, told a beautiful Welsh version. It seemed as thought this feat actually made it harder for some others to perform to the big audience. The competitive spirit had clearly been lurking, probably throughout both sessions, in spite of the fact that the group was a co-operative one.

I told my version twice in small groups and was able to tell it in a large one too, but felt impelled, each time, to say apologetically that the story was really too long for telling and needed more preparation. I was very much encouraged by the supportive responses I received from other people in the group and have since turned my notes into a written version (see Part 3, page 180).

5 Lasting Impressions

I may not have said enough to show that the overwhelming feeling of the sessions I have described was one of pleasure in sharing. First, there was the simple comfort and informality of sitting in a ring, centring on a common creative experience, which, for me, had symbolic importance, relating the occasion to some of my most enjoyable teaching experiences in English and drama lessons. There was a sense in which I felt a connection, too, with a older oral tradition, represented in my own life by a campfire singing and stories read to me as a child in the infant school, but going back beyond me into the distant past.

There was enormous enjoyment in witnessing the creation of a beautiful and touching story and savouring the way it worked by creating involvement, curiosity and suspense in all of us. There was a sad satisfaction in the ending of the story.

Above all, there was the release of creative energy expressed in writing which I found came about after the 'tasks' were set at the end of the first session. I found no shortage of ideas, either for the story or for the poem; if anything, there were too many ideas at first but, later, it became unusually easy to focus clearly on what I wanted to do and then to go ahead and do it. The shared listening, thinking and talking had so immersed me in Betty's story that I felt I knew it very well and was really aware of its metaphorical force by the time I was finally on my own and had to think about composing my own version.

Chapter 5
CONCLUSION

Old Tuscan proverb:
A tale is not beautiful if nothing is added to it.

Once upon a time there was an English teacher (secondary) who thought she would never be anything other than that. But she became a storyteller. No, not just an everyday storyteller like we all are, but a teller of magical tales. They were long tales, whole lesson-length ones. She told these tales to her streetwise teenage London lads, many of them big, cumbersome fellows, who made not a murmur or a movement while they listened. The science master said they had no manners, no language and no 'listening skills' but she knew he was wrong about all those things — she had the evidence — and wrong about the things he thought about them but didn't say. She was happy to be a storytelling English teacher (secondary) and thought she would never be anything else. But she was wrong about that, as you know by now. And you know how other teachers like her did similar and better things through storytelling, including reflecting upon the whole process and the significance of it all to learners of every age. These teachers are the kind of people from whom much could be learned about the realisation of human potential through language. They are putting it into practice for others and for themselves. And they are the ones best equipped to find out how to measure the success of what they are doing if it's testing that's required.

Now you have read about them, join them. Start storytelling now if you haven't already.

If you still have lingering doubts about the fundamental worth of the kind of work I have described here maybe it is because you prefer more authoritative voices. I'll include some here as a postscript for the faint-hearted.

It's not going to be easy, let me tell you (if I may be meta-narrativist for a moment). No, it isn't that I don't read the works of narratologists and such like because I do, sometimes. I discover all sorts of intriguing theories it would be interesting to put to you, but they wouldn't quite fit in this context as I shall explain. The ones I like best tend to be of the

"What oft was thought but ne'er so well expressed" kind and I am loath to suggest that something has more weight simply because it is said by a weightier person. However, I'll include one favourite of mine if you fancy further justification and a precedent for the retelling of tales:

[The value of a tale] *consists in what is woven and rewoven into it. I too have thought of myself as a link in the anonymous chain without end by which folk tales are handed down, links that are never merely instruments or passive transmitters but ... its real authors.*

Italo Calvino, introduction to *Italian Folk Tales* (Penguin 1982)

If a tale is good enough for Calvino ...

Another disadvantage for me at this point is that the writing of authority figures is often worded in a rather abstract way, quite unlike the style of Calvino above: by the time I have worked out what is meant I am also aware how such language can put classroom teachers off, not because it's irrelevant to what they are doing and thinking, or too difficult, but because teachers are very busy people. Here's a good example which I picked out recently and wanted to use:

... the narrative mode leads to conclusions not about certainties in an aboriginal world but about the varying perspectives that can be constructed to make experience comprehensible.

Jerome Bruner *Actual Minds, Possible Worlds* 1986

There's a prestigious academic for you, saying that the stories we meet are dependent on the experience which the reader/listener brings to bear upon them. Lesser academics often simply cannot escape the thesis-ese of their doctorate submissions. They dare not waste the evidence of the reading they have done to prove they are conversant with the field so quotations are uncomfortably stitched together. My book is not written to pass a university test but for teachers to read, follow and, I hope, believe. Publications born of higher-degree research are often weighted down with quotes and, while one part of me feels (unfairly) that there must be something suspect if so much back-up is necessary, another part of me is impressed to the extent that I shift fairly quickly to the back of the book to read the list of references to see if (a) I like the look of them and (b) if they are recent works — which is a bit silly, as though something written prior to the day before yesterday can't be right! I hope it is a bit silly since I shall shortly be referring to some research by psychologists working at the beginning of this century!

I remember reading the only one of the many reviews of *And None of it was Nonsense* which was rather less than enthusiastic throughout. (I was lucky and grateful to my publishers for all those free copies they sent to the right places!) It was written by a lecturer whose complaint, in patronising vein, was of a lack of theory in the book. This struck me as very odd. How could he have missed the 'theory' implied throughout the text itself? How did he fail to observe that then, as now, I am not engaging with others in a current specialised field of academic argument? Such is a perfectly respectable occupation but it isn't mine: I am communicating to practising teachers about what has come out of my own classroom. This is its own form of discipline for which I make no apology. A L Becker, concerned with the importance of particularity rather than theory, writes:

> ... one [way of] *working with a particular text grabs the theories as they come by and celebrates them by applying them and learning their lessons. But the discipline is not in the theories but in the particularities of the text — in context.*

and

> *Holding on to the experiences we have just shared is our discipline.*

In this respect, Jean Dunning's story of the workshop is the perfect exemplar. I am indeed interested in any theory which illuminates what has gone on in my own classrooms and workshops.

To return to the point, my main difficulty in picking choice quotations to underpin my text is that my book is not about doubtful arguments needing evidence but is about actual evidence itself, of premises I don't feel the least bit doubtful about! Years of experiencing the truth of them perhaps blinds me to possible demur from others. I must hunt around my text to discover why you, as a teacher, might still be unwilling to become a classroom storyteller. All the teachers' workshop chapters, to say the least, show our professional colleagues superbly in action. I shall do my best for you.

An interesting light is shed on retellings in an unusual book, *The Past We Share* by E L Ranelagh which demonstrates the way in which popular narratives from the East made their way into Europe and in the process inevitably became transformed in various ways. Ranelagh presents us with:

> *... the great float of folk narrative, often first recorded in India or Persia and thus classified as literature as well as folklore, but none the less primarily oral, which Arabic-speaking peoples shared and which they brought with them into Europe.*

He comments, when writing about the *Arabian Nights*:

> *Since the Nights are a composite work of separate tales told orally and over the course of many centuries, they have been — in Vance Randolph's immortal words — "shaped and polished by the natural hazards of oral transmission". Material is added or subtracted by chance and circumstance, but to survive a story must have the approval of audiences, who thus keep it and its teller on the rails. Millions over the years have thus supplied the shaping while the tellers supply the polish.*

Why not become one of the shapers and polishers? I say again, join us.

There is one area of hypothesis where I feel uneasy for a lack of theory. It is the claim that one is more truly oneself when telling and retelling stories than when one is using any other form of discourse, even including that which is composed entirely of statements about one's notion of oneself. This is of critical importance if your professional life has taught you, as it has me, that language development must be child-centred, person-centred, if it is to work; that people achieve their best when they are being truly themselves rather than copying or pleasing somebody else.

I went to the psychological research of Ebbinghaus and of Frederick Bartlett as described by Professor Ian Hunter, research which I understand has not been superseded since. It gives scientific evidence for the sort of statement I quoted from Bruner earlier. The research involved asking groups of subjects to listen to a folk tale and, after lapses of time of varying lengths, each subject retold the story as faithfully as possible to a new person, and he to another and so on. This is what Hunter reports in *Memory*:

Each person delineates in a way which seems important to him, which fits in with that unique background of cumulative past experience and those momentary attitudes which he inevitably brings to bear on his abstracting. In short, each person interprets the story in his own way ...

... [he] puts his own construction on the material as he listens to it. He interprets the incoming story in his own way, often unaware that he is doing so, that he is emphasising some features, ignoring others, perhaps reading into it what is not there. Each person abstracts a complex of characteristics which may differ from that abstracted by another person. This means that what different people retain will be different; and so too will be their subsequent retelling of the story.

The powerful difference between the retellings of folk stories undertaken by the subjects of these scientific experiments, and the retellings of pupils and teachers which I am concerned with in my work, is that the former were intended to be accurate reproductions of the 'original' whereas the latter are produced in a free atmosphere and will turn out to be as like or unlike the 'original' as the retellers, consciously or not, choose.

How much more so, then, in our activities with stories, will our individual lives, attitudes and cultures richly affect our interpretation and performance. It is enormously worthwhile and satisfying. Join us.

Let me finally say this. If nothing else, we share a desire to teach well by helping learners to learn. We live in times when the emphasis is not on how people learn but how they should be assessed. In all my decades of experience I have never once known a class of people, whatever their age or ability, achieve their best while being tested unless what is being tested isn't worth testing. Some individuals do, certainly, particularly those who confidently believe they are among the best performers in the group. But those same few, with all the rest, achieve best of all when they are doing something for and of themselves, something which makes dynamic sense of their own lives and their own way of seeing the world in which they live. This can happen with the stories we remember from our own lives, and stories we recollect which have been told by others throughout the history of humankind.

Until you begin to do it, you have scarcely any idea of the depth and width of your own memories. We all carry in our own heads enormous reserves of incident, of movements in time, of characters; even more exciting, we can have the power to make linkings, through words and images, between all this material from different times, and between it and the present, powers we never suspected before we began memory-diving, linkings which can delight by their often oddly revelatory rightness; apparently inexhaustible and endless process of discovery, largely but not entirely self-discovery.

A Sort of Clowning: Life and Times: 1940–59 by Richard Hoggart

Join us. Become a teller of tales. I will leave you with the tales.

Part 3 THE TALES

INTRODUCTION

1 The Land Where No One Ever Dies author's version

This was the first in a series of major stories which I told to two classes of 14/15-year-old boys over a period of one term, documented in *And None of it was Nonsense*. On the first two or three occasions when, having left full-time teaching, I went into primary and secondary schools as a 'storyteller', this was the story I felt safest taking with me. I quote it here for the latter reason and also because it is one of the stories in my repertoire that has become truly my own by dint of repeated tellings. Unlike several other stories which I tell, it no longer has any real connection with any text except the one my own head has constructed: Italo Calvino's version in his collection of Italian stories is like something I read a long time ago and can't quite recollect. I don't feel a sense of debt towards the collector himself — Calvino — but only towards that remarkable long-distance traveller called Folk Story. Again, unlike several other stories that I tell, this one has fully matured into a state which I'm happy about and I am unlikely to go on tinkering with it — except peripherally in adapting to the particular audience of the moment. It is useful to accumulate such stories, the real favourites. It's also important not to rely on them so much that one fails to accumulate new ones!

2 Death and Sweet William retold by Judith Baresel

I was introduced to the version upon which I base my own telling of this story — *Mr Death and the Red-headed Woman* — as one which the storyteller frequently used to help fatally ill children come to terms with their condition. *Death and Sweet William* is a retelling of a retelling of my own retelling of the tale!

A much less-sobering matter of speculation suggested by this story has

127

to do with accent and dialect. There are those who would claim that any story may be taken out of its cultural/linguistic context and told in a timeless, placeless way; or, even more drastic a change, it may be transposed by the teller into another culture altogether — one, perhaps, with which the teller herself or himself feels particularly comfortable (see *Chaim and the Chrane* below, originally from an Irish story). If such imaginative translation were not possible then how could stories travel successfully across time and space as they always have done and still do? Certainly a storyteller can succeed only when he or she feels the language of the telling rests easily upon the tongue. On the other hand, there is the kind of story which inhabits its own cultural garb so closely that the storyteller must either retain its 'original' idiom or leave it alone altogether. In this case, I could not bring myself to alter the American-ness of Mr. Death and his associates. Though I would not relish telling my version of this story in the presence of anyone from across the Atlantic, after much patient practice I am able to adopt an accent which is just sufficiently reminiscent of the American Wild West to keep me and most of my audience happy for most, sometimes all, of the time! I don't think there are any strong rules to be followed in such matters. What stays as it is in a story and what disappears from it is up to the storyteller concerned. The important thing is that while it is being told, the way it is told should seem to be the right way.

3 The Thieving Monkeys author's version

I first heard this at a NATE conference in Swansea told by the storyteller Godfrey 'Tuup'. An examination of this story as a resource is in *Story as Vehicle* by Edie Garvie. What you will read here is the transcription of my telling of this story in that Islington nursery which I refer to elsewhere as 'Rosalind's nursery'.

4 The Singing Drum author's version

I am grateful to Jane Grell, a storyteller based in Walthamstow, who told this story at a meeting of the London Narrative Group.

5 The Mice and the Fircones author's version

This story has proved very successful with small children who love to join in with the sound effects. I first heard it told in Calgary, Canada, by a kindergarten teacher, Jean Leonard. All three of these three stories have three things in common (besides being transcriptions of my own audio taped words on storytelling occasions at the pre-school centre where my youngest daughter works). First, they are all particularly well suited to telling to very young children and I have enjoyed the experience of telling them to 3- and 4-year-olds. Second, they do not bore me as do so many stories for infants; I am not particularly drawn to stories which are designed specifically for this age-group. I find myself especially averse to stories which involve conscious repetition of an idea or phrase over and over again because this is what is 'good' for children's language training! Third, the source of each story was an oral telling rather than a book. Told stories are so much more inviting than a story on a page, so it turns out that we storytellers are heavily mutually dependent for our inspiration!

6 The Bald, Warty Giant by Chris Stelling

7 The Giant Injection by Carol A Cooke

Both these stories were inspired by *The Giant over the Mountain* which I will tell to people of any age; on this occasion it was to a group of infant, primary and secondary teachers. The first one is embedded in the fairy story tradition compared with the modern setting of the second. Indeed, not only have we all had a giant injection experience but the precision of this account suggests straight autobiography (is there such a thing, I wonder, any more than there is any fantasy which is not born of real-life experience?).

Chris, a reception class teacher, wrote this of her story:

I told this story to my reception class as part of a topic on monsters. I read the children other monster stories, e.g. *Not Now, Bernard*, *Miranda's Monster* and *Where the Wild Things Are*. As a follow up the children made monsters out of collage material and pasta. They also made box model monsters. [Chris sent me a photograph of their quite amazing, high quality art work.]

The children made up their own stories about monsters and I was interested to hear them voice their own fears through the stories. They said that their monsters came out at night. One boy said that his monster lived in his wardrobe ...

8 Chaim and the Chrane by Harold Rosen

A Jewish story, this ... well, an ingenious Jewish retelling of a very Irish story, *The Man Who Had No Story*, in *Irish Folktales*, Penguin Folklore Library. Harold was much drawn to the Irish tale but felt uneasy about trying to transmit its essential Irishness, not least through the pronunciation of such place names as 'Barr an Ghaoith' and such person names as 'Brian O Braonachain'! He told the story, R P English with the inevitable touch of London about it; no place names and a hero called plain Brian; and an uncomfortable feeling on the part of the storyteller that something important had been lost. He told it at a NATE workshop we were running jointly in Leicester, during which he heard me do my Welsh version of *The Giant over the Mountain*. Thus an idea was born — an Irish story could be geographically transposed to a Jewish context, couldn't it? — and the result is a new story apparently straight out of London's East End earlier this century. Again, I wonder if it is really possible to make sharp distinctions between fact and fantasy ...

9 I Remember Ponty autobiography

Places — our own, that is — are incredibly capable of focusing memories of things past. The mere mention of a place that was familiar in some previous period of one's life, especially childhood, will cause a whole succession of images and impressions to flutter across the inward eye in an instant. For me, Tenby, Aberporth, Llangenerth, Abergavenny evoke a set of pictures each, which bears little or no connection with their picture-postcard representations and holiday brochures: they are pictures attached to events which took place during the earliest holidays away from home that I can remember.

Places are a rich source of stories in the classroom especially if it is multi-ethnic.

10 The Tale of Usheen author's version of *Usheen's Return to Ireland*, in *Irish Folktales* Penguin Folklore Library

11 The Fisherman and the Mermaid author's version of a Gaelic story

Both these stories are filled with enchantment for me and in the text I have chosen these two to demonstrate the way that hearing a story unleashes the creative powers of teachers (see Part 2, Chapters 1 to 4) as I have discovered on courses I have run. Usheen pursues the unattainable and, like another of my favourite characters, is removed from fantasy into the world of real life and death the moment his foot touches mother earth. The story of the fisherman seems to have travelled along the coast of Scotland — the tale of the woman who becomes the white silkie, the seal woman — and Ireland too, in many forms, the most beautiful for me being Seamus Heaney's retelling which, in turn, is a retelling of a version he heard from Sean O'Haughy in West Donegal.

12 The Fisherman and the Mermaid Jean Dunning's version

Jean gives her own account of the growth of her tale in Part 2, Chapter 4. I vividly remember her talking to me about the process she was going through when she was mulling over all her initial ideas. She said, and she meant it, that she felt she could write an entire novel based around this story. I know the feeling. Novels, like storytelling, are not something that only other people can produce.

The Land Where No One Ever Dies

In a village long, long ago — in northern Italy, I think it was — there lived a boy who knew everyone thereabouts and they all knew him. All the faces of the people were familiar. That's how it is in little villages, not at all like in cities. The seasons came and went. When the heavy rains fell the little stream that ran through the village scurried at a great rate, but when the sun beat down only a trickle was left to meander about among the hot, bald stones of the stream's bed. A stranger visiting the village from time to time would find everything pretty much the same from year to year. But things did not remain the same — nothing ever does. New life came into the world, people grew older — even wiser sometimes — and old folk shrank and died. That's just what happened one autumn evening to the boy's grandmother. Her death made the whole family mourn because they loved her very much, and she was especially precious to her favourite grandson.

The boy became very thoughtful. He decided that he wanted to stay in the world for longer than his grandmother had. He wanted to stay forever. "It seems," he thought, "from what people say and even from what I see for myself, that hereabouts death comes to everyone sooner or later." So he asked his parents what he could do about this. "There must be somewhere I could live forever."

"Oh no," said his mother and father, "there is nowhere. One day you must die like everyone else."

But this was no answer for the boy. He said, "I am going to try. There must be somewhere. There must be a land where no one ever dies and I am going to find it for myself."

He said goodbye to his mother and father, to his brothers and sisters, and he left all the neighbours, all his friends and relations to begin his long search. No one could help him, no one, until one day he came across an old man with a beard resting on his chest and this old man was pushing a wheelbarrow full of boulders and rubble. The boy greeted the old man and told him of his search. "I am looking for a land where no one ever dies. I do not want to die."

The old man said, "You could stay with me if you wish. You see that mountain?" He pointed towards a hillside nearby where there were many rocks and stones crumbling and tumbling down a steep slope. "I am moving the whole of it, spreading it over the plain, and one day that mountain will be level. You can stay and help me move its stones away and away. That will take a long time — only then will you die."

"How long will it take?" asked the boy.

"About a hundred years I would say."

"That won't do for me," replied the boy, and he took his leave of the old man and continued his journey.

In the distance he could see a vast forest. Soon he found himself swallowed up by its trees. There he came across an old man with a beard down to his middle and a large pruning knife in his right hand. "Good day to you, sir," said the boy, but the old man hardly looked up from his work, which seemed to be to prune back all the branches from a tree. "I wonder if you could help me," continued the boy. "I am trying to find a place where I can live forever."

"Then stay with me," replied the man. "You will die only when I have cleared away this whole forest."

"How long will that take?" asked the boy.

"Two hundred years or so, and I reckon no one but a madman would want to live longer than that."

"It's not long enough for me," said the boy and he went on his way.

After much travelling he reached a wide sea which disappeared over the edge of the distant horizon. He stood where the little grey waves lapped against the gravelly shore and gazed across the expanse of ocean. As he turned to walk on, he saw ahead of him the oldest man he had ever met in his life with a beard that came down to his very knees. The man's eyes were fixed upon a duck which, at his feet, was drinking from the little waves that trickled over the coarse sand, lapping up the water of the ocean into his flat beak. The boy asked his question yet again. "Can you help me, sir? I am looking for the land where I will never die."

"This spot is surely good enough for you. I am waiting for the day when this little duck has drunk the whole ocean dry. Stay with me and only then will you die."

"How long will that take?" asked the boy.

"I would guess three hundred years. At the end of such a time you will be tired enough of life and ready to move on."

"No, no," replied the boy, "I must go on with my search. I do not want to die at all, not ever." And with that he left.

Farther off from the great ocean he could see a high mountain. As he came nearer he saw there was a castle on the top of it and a little track that wound its way up to its entrance. He stared at the twisting road and at the castle swathed in shifting clouds and he had a feeling in his bones that his journey was soon to end.

His pace quickened and soon he was climbing up the ragged path, over the stones and potholes. It was a long, slow haul up that winding way and beside the road were muddy ditches. Eventually he reached the oaken door of the castle and banged upon it as loudly as he could with his small fist. He heard footsteps from within. The door slowly, stiffly creaked open. There, framed in the doorway was the oldest man you could imagine, his grey beard reaching right down to his feet.

"Can you help me?" asked the boy. "I am looking for a place where no one ever dies."

"You have come to the right place," said the old man. "You have reached your journey's end. This indeed is the place where no one ever dies. This is the place where you can live forever. Come in, do. I would be glad of some company for I am here all alone." So he went into the castle and the great door swung to behind him.

At last the boy was content. Time passed. He and the old man kept each other company and many a tale was told between them.

One morning, when the sun rose and a slight breeze blew in through his bedroom window, he was suddenly reminded of the little bedroom where he had slept as a child and he was overcome by a great longing to see his own village again and to look into his mother's eyes. He wanted to see his whole family, his brothers and sisters, the neighbours — all the people who had shared his life, had comforted him in his troubles and had laughed and played with him in the sunshine.

He went to the old man and said, "Could you help me again? It is good being here with you but I would just like to have one look at he village where I was born and maybe pass the time of day with some of the neighbours and remind myself of my mother's face."

The old man frowned and said, "But you chose to come here. You chose the land where no one ever dies."

The boy sighed. "Just once I would like to go back. I really would like to see them. I'll come back when I've done."

"Very well. If that is your choice go to the stable, mount the white stallion and ride like the wind until you get back to your own village and then return. But take heed of this. Whatever happens, do not dismount. Stay on the horse until you are inside this castle once again for if you put one foot on the earth you are doomed."

The boy did what he was told. He rode down the mountain road and off the way he had once travelled. Soon he came to a huge marsh and he saw nearby a heap of bones and a little pile of feathers. He realised that this was where there had once been a great sea but the duck had long since drunk it dry. He did not get off his horse but rode on like the wind and soon came to a barren land where the wind tossed swirls of dust and an occasional dead stump pointed a wooden claw out of the ground. This had once been a green forest. He rode on and on. The land stretched flat and bare ahead with not a hill in sight. Once there had been a mighty mountain in those parts but it had been laid low and all its rocks and soil carried off in a wheelbarrow. At least he knew he was not far from home. He came to a village where there was something familiar about the curve of the main street and the angle of a stream that ran beside it. Suddenly he realised that this was where his own village had once stood. But the stone houses had all gone and brick buildings replaced them. He turned his horse towards the lane where his own home used to be but there was nothing of it to be seen but for a few scattered and broken blocks of stone. He rode back to the centre of the village. People passed him from time to time but their faces were unfamiliar and they did not look up at the boy on the big white horse. There was nothing for it but to go back the way he had come, so with a heavy heart he turned and galloped away from that place of strangers.

He rode hard, past the plain of rubble where there had once been a mountain, past the sandy desert where there had once been a forest and past the soggy marsh where the waves of the sea had once flowed towards the shore. When he reached the mountain road which led to the castle he could see ahead what seemed to be a cart with a lumpy load about half way up the slope. He discovered when he reached it that it was tilted because one of its wheels had slipped down the mud into the ditch at the side of the road and an old man was vainly struggling to right the cart which was full of old boots and shoes. "Help me, please. It is nearly dusk and I cannot pull my cart out of the ditch before nightfall by myself," said the old fellow.

"I'm sorry, I cannot help you," replied the boy. "I have to stay on my horse."

"Oh, please have pity on an old man! Your limbs are young and strong. You could pull my cart back on the road in no time at all. What does one moment matter to someone who has all his life to come?"

Perhaps the man was right, thought the boy. After all, he had nothing but life ahead so could surely spare a little of it now. He swung his leg over the horse's back and his foot touched the earth.

"Got you! Got you at last!" cried the man, gripping the boy by his wrist. "I have travelled the whole world looking for you. See all the boots and shoes I have worn out in my search? I am Death. No one escapes my clutch."

And the boy died there and then.

Author's version

Death and Sweet William

One day Sweet William came riding into town. Sweet William was a cowboy and he was riding his strawberry roan mare, Rosa. Sweet William thought Rosa the finest horse in the west and wouldn't sell her for any money; he said she loved him more like a lover than a horse and she wouldn't let anyone but him ride her. So here came Sweet William riding into town on Rosa to see his sweetheart, Maud Applegate, with a pocketful of money because he'd just been paid, and life seemed pretty good to him.

Before Sweet William reached Maud Applegate's house he had to pass Nellie Janssen's saloon, and he thought he'd just stop off and have a drink with Nellie and maybe a word with one or two of the boys — though why Sweet William should want to stop off with Nellie Janssen when Maud Applegate was waiting for him is more than I can say. But he jumped off Rosa, wrapped the reins round the rail and climbed the board steps to the saloon.

But what Sweet William didn't know was that in Nellie Janssen's saloon Dead Eye Dick was waiting for him. Now Dead Eye Dick hated Sweet William, and when he saw him come in he pulled out his gun and aimed at Sweet William. Sweet William, he pulled out his gun too, and they both fired. Sweet William's shot went wide and all it broke was some of the bottles behind the bar so there was glass and liquor all over the saloon, and Nellie Janssen squawking; but Dead Eye Dick shot true, and there was Sweet William lying on the floor of Nellie Janssen's saloon with his life's blood pouring out of him.

Now while all this was going on Maud Applegate was on the back porch of her house churning butter. She was wearing a homespun skirt and an old man's shirt with the sleeves turned up to the elbow, she'd no shoes on and her hair was hanging in a plait down her back, but for all this she looked as fresh and sweet as an apple blossom. When she heard the two shots ring out somehow she knew, don't ask me how, that it was Sweet William that had been shot. She dropped the plunger and ran out into the road, bare-footed as she was, and started towards Nellie Janssen's saloon as fast as she could go.

As she ran she heard the sound of mighty hooves coming up behind her, and she turned and saw a great grey horse with a shadowy figure on it riding towards her and she knew this was Death coming to carry off Sweet William. Well, she managed to run just a little faster and reached the saloon at the same time as the great grey horse. She looked up at the shadowy figure and said, "Oh Death, don't you take Sweet William from me, because he's the only living man on this earth as I can ever marry, and if you take him seems to me I'll die an old maid!"

Death, he looked down at Maud, standing there as sweet and as fresh as apple blossom, and said, "Well, see here Maud Applegate, I wouldn't do this for everyone, but seeing it's you I'll let him have one more day so that you can say goodbye properly. But don't you come back to me tomorrow asking for more time; one day is all you'll get!" And he wheeled his great grey horse and galloped back the way he'd come.

Maud looked after him and then, instead of going into the saloon she went up to Rosa, unhitched her and climbed up into the saddle. Rosa wasn't wearing a side-saddle, and Maud had to pull her skirt up to her knees, but strange to say Rosa didn't seem to mind Maud riding her — maybe she understood it was for Sweet William's sake. And Maud turned Rosa's head and they galloped off after Death on his great grey horse.

Well Rosa was a good horse and a willing horse, but there was no way she could catch up Death on his great grey horse. Nevertheless, Maud managed to keep them in sight and she rode for a long time after Death along a strange and lonesome road. At last the road came to an end at an old ranch-house. Maud could see no sign of Death or his horse so she climbed down from Rosa and knocked on the door of the ranch-house.

Out came an old old woman, and Maud said, "How dye do ma'am! I'm Maud Applegate. Can you tell me where I can find Death?"

"Now what's a sweet young thing like you doing looking for Death?"

"Why he wants to take Sweet William from me, who's the only living man on this earth as I can ever marry, and if he takes him seems to me I'll die an old maid. I want to know how I can stop him."

"Well see here, Maud Applegate, this is Death's ranch up back of the stars, and I'm his granny and he's out the back doing the chores. Now here's what I'll do for you. I'll ask Death three questions for you, and you can hide in the kitchen where you can hear his answers. You picket your horse over there where Death can't see her — ain't nobody going to steal her from Death's ranch — and you can be thinking what questions you want me to ask for you."

Maud picketed Rosa out of sight, and then came back to the ranch. Death's granny said, "Have you thought what questions you want me to ask for you, Maud?"

"My first question is how I can stop Death taking Sweet William away from me ever — I'll tell you my other questions later if that's agreeable to you ma'am."

Death's granny hid Maud behind the salt pork barrel in the corner of the kitchen, and soon Death came in carrying a load of firewood. "Come in and sit down, grandson, and I'll give you your supper," said the old woman.

"What sort of a day did you have?" she said, ladling beans on to his plate.

"Well," said Death, starting to eat, "it was a funny sort of day. I was bound to fetch Sweet William, as he was shot in a saloon bar shoot-out, but his sweetheart, Maud Applegate, she asked me so nicely to give him more time, I said he could have one more day. Don't know if I did the right thing but there it is." And he finished the beans on his plate and put down his spoon.

"Ain't there no way you could fix not taking Sweet William at all?" she said, piling on some more beans.

"Well, see here Granny," said Death, picking up his spoon again, "you know as well as I do that wouldn't be no kindness. Time would come when Sweet William, he'd be hollering for me to come and take him; ain't no way I'd agree to that, and it would be unprofessional if I did. But I'd give him another fifty years, that's as much as any man in his senses would want, if Maud Applegate would ride with me stirrup to stirrup all day tomorrow and then give me a smacking kiss." Now Maud she heard all this, and now she knew all she needed to know.

But it seemed to her it would be impolite not to ask the other questions when they'd been offered to her, so when Death's granny came across to the stove to take out an apple pie, she leaned out from behind the salt pork barrel and whispered to the old woman, "Ask him why he took my little sister, who was so pretty and sweet and good." So Death's granny said as she cut a slice from the pie and put it before Death "How come you took Maud Applegate's little sister, who was so pretty and sweet and good?"

"Well," said Death, taking a mouthful of the pie, "the fact is she was so tired and weak, she was real happy to come with me." Maud heard this and thought of her little sister and remembered how tired and weak she was before Death took her, and thought maybe Death was right, her little sister wasn't sorry to go with him.

Maud couldn't think of another question to ask, so in the end as Death's granny came to the stove again to take out a blueberry pie she leaned out and whispered "Ask him what he does when he's not fetching folks." Death's granny carried the blueberry pie back to the table and said to him as she cut a slice for him, "See here, grandson, what do you do when you're not fetching folks?"

And Death, he just toyed with the pie and looked kind of sad and said, "Nothing much, but sometimes at nightfall I goes up to folks' houses and looks in at the mammy and pappy and little children sitting round the table in the lamplight and I think how happy they look." And he sighed and took a mouthful of pie.

Soon after that Death finished the slice of blueberry pie and went off to his bed and Maud came out from behind the salt pork barrel. Death's granny gave her some supper and made her up a bed on the floor in front of the stove and there she spent the night.

The next morning when Death mounted his great grey horse, there was Maud waiting for him, riding Rosa. Rosa still hadn't got a side-saddle and Maud was still riding with her homespun skirt tucked up round her knees, but for all that she looked as sweet and as fresh as apple blossom. Death looked at her and said, "Seems to me like someone's been listening at doors," but he said no more and rode off on his great grey horse along the strange and lonesome road. Maud rode after him on Rosa, and though she couldn't quite catch him up, and though Rosa seemed kind of scared of the great grey horse, she kept up pretty well.

After a bit she said, "Where are we going, Death?" and Death replied, "We're off to the big woods. There's a young boy there has climbed a tree and he's going to fall off and then I'm bound to take him."

"What!", said Maud, "A little young boy! What about his mammy and pappy? Have you thought how they'll feel if you take him? You mustn't do it, Death!"

"Ain't nothing I can do about it. If he falls out of that tree I'm bound to take him."

They rode on, but when they came to the big woods and near the tree Maud kicked Rosa and managed to overtake Death and the great grey horse. She jumped off Rosa and threw the reins over a branch before Death came up, and started to climb the tree, calling, "I've come to help you! Now just you stay where you are until I come up and help you down." And when she climbed up near the little young boy she guided his feet down, bit by bit, until she had him safe on the ground. He looked at her, gave one frightened glance at Death and ran off.

Death said, "Seems to me you've saved me some work," but he waited while she remounted Rosa and they rode off together. Maybe it was just that she'd got her wind, but it seemed to Maud that Rosa kept up better with the great grey horse than she had before and didn't seem so scared of him. They rode on a long time before Maud said, "Where are we going now, Death?"

"We're off to the Southern States. There's a lynching party out just about to string up a black man, and then I'll be bound to take him."

"A lynching party? What for are they stringing up the black man?"

"Ain't my business and I don't know. For being black, I guess."

Well Maud, she didn't say any more, but when they come up near the lynching party she took a pin from her shirt and stuck it hard into the hindquarters of the great grey horse. Well the great grey horse wasn't used to this sort of treatment and he reared up high, and the lynching party they took one look at death on his rearing horse and ran off as hard as they could go. Just the black man remained behind, and he couldn't run because he was tied up. Maud got down from Rosa, tossed the reins to Death to hold and untied the black man, who looked at her and at Death and said, "Why thank you most kindly ma'am. Seems to me you've saved my life, and I'm deeply grateful." And he too took one frightened look at Death and he ran off, but in a different direction from the lynching party.

Maud she remounted Rosa and they rode on, and now it was quite clear Rosa was keeping up well with the great grey horse and didn't seem scared of him at all. After a bit Maud said, "Where are we going now, Death?"

"We're off to the Great Lakes. There's a poor silly young woman about to drown herself and her little babby."

Well, Maud she didn't say anything to this, and Death looked round at her, and said in alarm, "Now see here, Maud Applegate, I ain't fixing to take you off today! It ain't time for that. Don't you go drowning yourself trying to save this poor silly woman!"

"Ain't no question of my drowning. I've been able to swim like a fish ever since I was so high."

Well, when they came up to the lake, Death he put out his hand for Rosa's reins, it seems he was getting to know it wasn't any use his trying to stop Maud Applegate when she'd set her mind on something, and Maud ran into the lake and swam out to where the poor silly young woman and her little baby were just about to drown and she hauled them back to the shore.

The young woman looked at her in wonder, and said, "Who are you, and how do you dare to travel with Death?"

Maud replied, "Well see here, honey, I'm Maud Applegate and I'm riding stirrup to stirrup with Death all day to save Sweet William, because he's the only living man on this earth as I can ever marry, and if he dies seems to me I'll die an old maid! But honey, what are you trying to kill yourself and that sweet babby? You just hang on and you'll find things come all right in the end."

"Well Maud, I'm just a hired girl and my master turned me out when I had this babby. I ain't got no husband, and I ain't got no family neither and it seemed to me I just couldn't manage. But it was mighty brave the way you pulled me and the babby out of the water and I reckon it's a mighty brave thing you're doing riding with Death, and when I see how brave you are, seems to me maybe I ought to carry on a bit longer."

"That's right, honey, and just you wait and see, that babby of yours will grow up a real credit to you. Ain't that so, Death?" said Maud.

"That's so," answered Death. "If I don't take that babby today he'll grow up and he'll be a famous doctor, and there's many and many folks as I won't take till they're old old men and women all on account of him."

"That's great to hear," said the young woman, "knowing that I reckon I can keep going. Thank you kindly for telling me. And thank you, Maud Applegate, for saving me and babby today."

Well, this time Death helped Maud into the saddle and they rode off.

"Where are we going now, Death?"

"Back to the ranch up back of the stars; I ain't got no more work to do today."

Along they rode, quite friendly and companionable, and night was falling when they saw a light in a little shanty. Death rode up to the shanty, and Maud rode with him.

"Why are you going here, Death? I thought you had no more work to do today."

"That's right, I've no more work lined up, but I just want to look in the window; I won't take nobody." So the two of them rode up to the window and looked in. It was a poor shanty, but the lamp was lit on the table and round it were sitting a man and a woman and four little children and they were eating their supper and looking real content with each other.

"It looks real homely in there," said Death. "That man must sure be a happy man I reckon." He gave a sort of sigh.

Maud looked and said, "That is so. And I reckon that's a happy woman there." And she too gave a sort of sigh.

Well they rode back along the strange and lonesome road until it was almost dark and at last they reached the ranch up back of the stars. Maud said, "Death, I've ridden with you stirrup to stirrup all day, and now you must leave Sweet William with me for fifty years."
"Ain't you forgotten one thing, Maud Applegate? Seems to me there was a kiss mentioned."

She got down from Rosa and stood there with her eyes closed waiting for him to kiss her.

"No, Maud Applegate, it was for you to kiss me, not contrariwise."

So she went up to him and flung her arms round Death and hugged him and gave him a long and smacking kiss, and he put his arms round her and hugged her ... but it was Death who slackened his hug before Maud Applegate did.

When Maud finally let Death go, Death's granny, who was standing at the door of the ranch-house looking at them, called out, "Say there, Maud Applegate, why don't you come in and freshen up and maybe have a bite of supper and stay the night?" Now Maud had been through a lot that day — she'd ridden all day, she'd climbed a tree and she'd been in a lake, her clothes had been wet and dried on her, her skirt was torn, her hair was full of pine needles and waterweed, and taken all in all she wasn't quite as fresh and as sweet as she'd been when she started out. But she didn't care and she replied, "Oh no, thank you kindly ma'am. I've got to get back to Sweet William because he's the only living man on this earth as I can ever marry, and if I don't marry him seems to me I'll die an old maid!"

So she climbed back on to Rosa and started towards the strange and lonesome road. But soon she became aware that Death was riding beside her on his great grey horse. "See here Death," she said, "I thought you said you'd let Sweet William have fifty more years. Why are you riding back to town?"

"That is so, and I ain't one to go back on my promises. But do you think I would let a lady ride along along the strange and lonesome road? No sirree, I'm riding with you to take care of you." And they rode back to town, along the strange and lonesome road, very friendly and companionable, and the road didn't seem long to either of them.

Well when they got to town Maud jumped down from Rosa, flung the reins over the rail, turned and waved to Death and ran up the steps into the saloon. Death looked after her, then turned the head of his great grey horse and started back the way he'd come, kind of slow and weary. But as he rode he suddenly heard the sound of hooves behind him, and looking back he saw Maud Applegate riding after him on Rosa as hard as she could go. "See here, Maud Applegate," he said as she came up, "what are you coming back for? Sweet William's all right isn't he?"

"Don't you talk to me about that lowdown sneaking skunk! I reckon Stinking Billy would be a better name for him than Sweet William! And if I weren't a lady there's stronger language I could use about that two-faced slimy rattlesnake!"

"Why Maud, what did he do to you?"

"He said I'd stolen Rosa and that he'd have the sheriff after me! And he said I looked a mess! And he's going to marry that no-good Nellie Janssen! Waaaah!" And she started to cry.

"But see here, Maud Applegate, I thought Sweet William was the only living man on this earth as you could ever marry, and if you didn't marry him you'd die an old maid!"

Maud cried a little longer, then looked at Death and a light came into her eyes, "Why Death, seems to me you ain't no living man, and the ranch up back of the stars sure ain't on this earth, and if I were to marry you seems to me there ain't no reason to think I'd die an old maid!"

Well Death had learnt one thing that day, and that was that it was no manner of use his trying to gainsay Maud Applegate if her mind was set on something — and maybe he didn't want to either. So they rode back along the strange and lonesome road to the ranch up back of the stars, he on his great grey horse and she on Rosa, very quiet and loverlike in the starry night.

When they reached the ranch up back of the stars, Death's granny had seen the way things were shaping and she'd prepared a fine wedding breakfast for them and asked the preacher to look by to see that they were properly wed. And the last I heard of them, Death and Maud Applegate were living together at the ranch up back of the stars, very happily with Death's granny and four fine young children. But while Death likes nothing better than to go out riding with Maud, he won't take her with him when he's working; he says she's bad for trade.

Judith Baresel

The Thieving Monkeys

There was a certain place in Africa where people from miles and miles around would go to the market to buy their goods. And people would go there to sell things as well as to buy. Now I've brought with me some of the things that people liked to buy and sell in that market. My best friend from over there, called Yowi, went there every week ... but let me show you some of the things you could see on the stalls there if you went. Just look at these clothes. And this beautiful cloth. See? That's something that everybody liked and everybody wanted to buy but he kept it for me because I'm his friend. Now I'm going to make a market stall over here. Yes. On this table. So you put that material across the table, go on.

Now what else have I got for the market stall? Let's see. *[Plenty of comments from children as they saw and touched the items.]* Just look at this — a woven basket. Sandals. See that statue? Some people there were brilliant at carving. A wooden spoon and fork — I use them when we have salad. And bowls. And these beads. Just look. All on to the market table.

Now here's a hat. See? Do I look good in it? Well, Yowi had lots of hats like this. He used to put them in this great big basket and take them to market. This basket was full of hats when he left home early in the morning and he'd go to the market (over there) from his home (over here) and walk all — this — long — walk — until — at — last — he — got to the market stall (over here).

Right, now I'll tell you about Yowi and what happened to him. Every week he'd go to the market with his big basket full of hats. Look. Here it is, full of hats. He'd sell all these hats and he'd go all the way home along the jungle path with money in his pocket, very pleased with himself.

Sometimes on his way to market early in the morning he'd be in the middle of the jungle and he'd feel a bit hungry and thirsty so he'd open his little shoulder bag and take out some fruit to eat, juicy fruit that would quench his thirst as well. And do you know, as soon as he'd got it out, all the monkeys would come down from the trees to have a look at Yowi and his fruit. They'd sit around and their tongues would be hanging out because they fancied Yowi's fruit, too. So Yowi would often share his fruit with the monkeys. Do you want a bit of my fruit? Little monkey, do you want some fruit? *[children have some ...].* All the monkeys were very pleased with Yowi. What a nice fellow, they thought, he shares his things with us. Do you want a grape from the hat-seller? Didn't you get one before? Right. They're really nice, they haven't got any pips.

So Yowi would leave his house ... over here, and he walked and walked his way towards the market through the jungle. It was a long way through the jungle to the market and the monkeys up in the trees saw Yowi coming, and they chattered to each other: he's coming-he's coming-he's coming-he's coming, they whispered and muttered together. They all came down from the trees and you'll never believe what they did! They leapt out of the trees and ... they took his hats! They took all of Yowi's hats!

You take one, go on. *[Children take the 'hats'.]* Yes, all the hats went. You don't want one? Well, the other monkeys all wanted a hat and they put the hats on their heads! Yes, go on then, take one for your friend ...

And Yowi looked into his basket and ALL the hats had gone! He'd got no hats! No hats to sell in the market!

Yowi felt very cross with the monkeys. He said, "Monkeys, you give me back my hats!" *[Chorus of nos.]* But they wouldn't — the monkeys kept the hats on their heads. So Yowi said again, "Monkeys, you give me back my hats!" *[Children shout, "no!".]*

You see? They all had the hats on and they wouldn't take their hats off.

Yowi was very cross. "You are very bad monkeys," he said and he shook his fist at them. And the monkeys shook their fists back at Yowi. This made him crosser so he shook his fist again. And the monkeys shook their fists at him again *[children shake their fists at storyteller.]* This made him even crosser and he put his tongue out rudely at the monkeys *[children respond, etc.].* ... This made him even crosser so he pulled a really ugly face at the monkeys and they pulled one back ... This made him even crosser so he shook both his fists in the air at the monkeys.

Yowi was so cross that he took off his hat and he threw it on the ground, like that.

And all the monkeys-took-off-their-hats-and THREW-them on the ground, too.

As soon as Yowi saw what they had done he rushed around as fast as he possibly could picking up all the hats they had thrown down, every single one of them! And he went to the market ... (over here) with his hats and he sold the lot to the people, and he went back home afterwards
through the jungle, ha,ha,ha,
through the jungle, ha,ha,ha,
through the jungle, ha,ha,ha,
very happy, jangling his money in his pockets. He waved to the monkeys as he passed them and they waved back. But he made sure that he never ever let the monkeys take his hats again.

Author's version

The Singing Drum

In the middle of the village the two little sisters played in and out, round, about, here, there and everywhere, everywhere that they'd played many and many a time before. But Bimwili did not play with them. Their little sister Bimwili did not play with them that day because they had told her they did not want her with them. Bimwili had cried and felt lonely. Bimwili often felt lonely because she had a lame foot. Her lame foot slowed her down. She did not have two strong limbs like her sisters and everybody else did. Bimwili was born with a difference. When she was born her mother cried to see her twisted foot. When she was two Bimwili still hadn't learned to walk on it. Now she was five her sisters wanted to run fast in their games so they often played without her.

But Bimwili didn't often cry and her mother had ceased to cry about Bimwili's twisted foot as soon as Bimwili had smiled her first smile. She was in fact a very happy child who played a lot with her sisters and with other children in the village. Even when their games were too fast for her, Bimwili soon found other things to do by herself because she was that kind of person. Sometimes she made necklaces out of melon seeds. Sometimes she helped her mother to gather fruit. Sometimes she drew patterns in the earth with a fat stick. Sometimes she went to the well to draw water for the family.

It was very early in the morning and her sisters came from their play just as soon as Bimwili had dried her tears and begun thinking about what she would do next. They went straight up to their mother and said, "We feel in the mood for an adventure today. We want to walk the whole length of the jungle path until we reach the sea."

"That's a long way," said their mother, "but you could all get there by the time the sun is high if you set off now."

"Both of us, not all of us," said Bimwili's older sister.

"Then you cannot go," said their mother, "and that's that."

The sisters wanted to go very badly so they decided to take Bimwili. They strolled along the jungle path, listening to the screeching parrots and the chattering monkeys, thoroughly enjoying their freedom. By the time they glimpsed the sea between the trunks of the trees and the hanging lianas the sun was hot on their heads and the children were ready to cool their bodies in the sea. Bimwili's sisters were leaping in and out of the waves long before she herself reached the water's edge but she was so happy to feel the sand under her feet and to see the great gleaming stretch of water before her that she did not mind in the least that they had raced off without her.

She found little pearl shells on the beach and tiny crab creatures scurrying about. Suddenly a wave rose high up ahead and tossed something towards her, something as big as a mango, pink and shiny. It rolled up the beach in the swirl at the tip of the wave then rested, still as a stone, on the wet sand while the waters slipped back from it. Bimwili picked it up. It was a creamy colour with pale yellowy brown ridges, like the ribbed wet sand. She turned it over. The inside of the shell, where it kept its secrets, was silken smooth, and pink like a peach. Bimwili placed its open edge to her ear and she heard the whispering of the wind over the oceans where the shell had been and the sighing of the waves that had carried it to her. Bimwili thought the shell was the most wonderful thing she had ever seen.

She called her sisters who came over to see what Bimwili was holding in her hand. "It's really beautiful," they said. "You're a very lucky girl." When her sisters had gone back into the water Bimwili placed the shell carefully on a big rock and stepped back to admire it from a distance. She began to play in the sand by herself and while she played she made up a song about the shell. It went like this.

> I have a shell from out of the sea
> A shell the big wave gave to me
> It's pink inside like the sunset sky
> If I listen, I hear the ocean sigh.

She sang it over and over and was still singing when her sisters appeared in front of her to tell her it was time to go. Each of them took her by the hand and between them they helped Bimwili to walk along the path more quickly than when they had come that way earlier.

Suddenly Bimwili realised she had left her shell behind on the rock. "We can't go back now, it's too late," her sisters said. But Bimwili would not go home without her shell so her sisters left her to fetch it herself and make the journey home alone.

Bimwili felt afraid on the jungle path by herself and she sang her shell song over and over to give herself courage. When she reached the beach the rocks cast long shadows. They looked like crouching animals. Bimwili sang her song brightly as she limped towards the rock where she had placed her shell. But something else, something much bigger, was also on the rock. There, sitting with her shell beside it, was the Zimwi.

The Zimwi was long and wrinkly and hairy like a coconut. His fingers hung down at the end of his long arms like wooden twigs. "What are you doing here, little girl?" the Zimwi asked.

"I've come for my shell," Bimwili whispered.

"Come up beside me," said the Zimwi in a croaky, wheedling way, "and sing your song again and then I'll give you your shell."

Bimwili did what she was told. The very moment she sang the last word of her song the Zimwi reached out with his skinny arm, grabbed Bimwili and bundled her into a big drum which was open beside him on the sand, then he put the lid on it, shutting her inside. "You can stay in there," cried the Zimwi, "and every time I beat on the drum, you must sing the song for me else you'll get nothing to eat."

At that very same moment, back in the village the two sisters arrived home. Their mother could not believe her eyes when she saw Bimwili was not with them. She was very angry and very, very upset. In no time her friends and neighbours gathered and a search party went into the jungle to bring Bimwili home, out of the darkness which was gathering around them. They searched all that night and all next day. They went on searching for many days and in their heads they remembered Bimwili and how much they loved her. But Bimwili was inside the Zimwi's drum. He carried her on his back from village to village, telling the people to come and listen to his magic singing drum. People thought it was marvellous when they heard the drum's song. That way the Zimwi got lots of praise and smiles from the people and plenty of tasty things to eat. But at the end of each day the Zimwi went off with his drum into the jungle and only then did he open his drum to let Bimwili have something to eat — berries and bananas and coconut from the jungle itself.

The day came when the Zimwi arrived at Bimwili's own village. "Gather under the mango tree," cried the Zimwi, "and listen to my magic singing drum."

The people came to see what was what. The Zimwi beat on the drum and Bimwili began to sing. By now she had changed her song but the Zimwi hadn't noticed that now she sang of her sorrow.

I had a shell from out of the sea
A shell the Zimwi stole from me
It's dark in here like the midnight sky
If you listen, you'll hear Bimwili cry.

Bimwili's two sisters looked at each other. Their eyes said, "That's Bimwili's voice!"

They scuttled away to tell their mother what they had heard. Their mother hurried to join the crowd that had gathered around the Zimwi and his drum. She listened carefully.

I had a shell from out of the sea
A shell the Zimwi stole from me
It's dark in here like the midnight sky
If you listen, you'll hear Bimwili cry.

"Let me get you something to eat, Mr Zimwi" said her mother. "Would you like fish or fowl with your rice?"

"Fish. Fish," replied the Zimwi.

"Then could you fetch me water from the well?" said Bimwili's mother.

"Yes. Yes," said the Zimwi.

As soon as he was out of sight they rushed to the drum and took off the lid. There she was! There she was at last! But there was not much time for joy and kisses just then. As quickly as they could they carried Bimwili back to her home and the neighbours put stones in the drum. When the Zimwi returned and went back to his drum, the people laughed and scoffed at him, for however much he beat his drum there was no magic singing to be heard at all.

Much later that evening, alone in the jungle, the Zimwi discovered the trick they had played on him; he howled with fury and stamped his skinny foot. Never, never did he go back to the village where Bimwili and her sisters played, always happy, always glad to be together.

Author's version

The Mice and the Fircones

Once upon a time, a long, long time ago in a place called North America, there weren't any people at all with skin the same colour as mine. All the people in North America had rosy brown skin and they all lived together and were very happy because nobody came to disturb or hurt them. They lived in houses like tents, called tepees, and the ones I'm going to tell you about had the prettiest tents of all because these human beings that I am telling you about had decided to stay on one particular piece of land, rather than to move their tents from place to place. All round the tall tents, the tepees, where they lived there were great big trees, pine trees like huge Christmas trees. And the wind would come and would blow in the pine trees and the pine trees would whisper together — shwshwshwshwshw ... The people inside the tents could hear the pine trees whisper — shwshwshwshwshw ...

And in the summer time they could hear the corn whispering. These Indians grew corn. Look, I've brought some to show you. Let's see if I can find it in my bag. I bought it in Muswell Hill before I came this morning. Here it is, my piece of maize, which the Indians grew hundreds and hundreds of years ago. I bought it from a man with a barrow. Some people call it sweetcorn; some people call it maize; some people call it corn on the cob ...

In the spring, the little tiny plants of corn would start pushing their way through the earth where the human beings had planted the seeds of corn. The sun would shine, the rains would come and the stems of the corn would grow longer. And out on the sides of the stem would grow the ears of corn — little ones like this one, with the unripe corn inside — look, I'll peel the leaves off. This is what they'd find inside when the corn was ripe in the summer — lovely golden grains of corn ... yes, a hairy top to it, all silky ... *[children say, "My mummy cooks that"... big chorus of voices ...]*

Well, once upon a time, the little Indian children as big as you would go out into the field and they would look at the corn each day and when it was ripe they'd rush to tell their mums and dads "The corn is ripe! The corn is ripe! We can pick it now!"

Now one day, when the corn was nearly, almost ripe, the children heard a tiny little sound in the corn. They heard a little rustling, a pattering, a scurrying, a scuttling, a twitching and a scratching of little tiny feet. What was it? What could it be, they thought? They peered into the corn. Do you know what they saw? They saw hundreds and hundreds of tiny little mice, running along the earth, scurrying up the stalks, digging their twitching whiskers and noses under these long leaves. The corn was covered in little mice, little mice had come rustling on their tiny pattering feet into the plain and they'd run around the bottom of the corn stems, and climbed up the corn stalks and onto the corn cobs and they'd started nibbling at the corn! There were hundreds of little mice!

The children looked at each other and they said, "What will happen to us? What will we have to eat in the winter if the mice eat all the corn? We'll have no dinner or tea or supper and we'll die of hunger!" So they ran back to the tepees, the tents where their parents were and they told their news. "Come quick to the corn fields! The mice have come to eat up all our food! Come quick! The corn is covered with little mice!"

"It can't be!" said the mummies and daddies.

"Oh yes it is," said the children, because they had seen it for themselves, and they dragged their mummies and daddies after them, "Come and see!" and all the people, all the human beings came to the corn.

There they saw ... little tiny feet on the corn; little tiny teeth in the corn, nibble, nibble. And — the — people — all — stood — up — and — they — raised — their — arms — towards — the — sky, and they called out in a loud voice, "Oh, great god of the skies, we will share our corn with the mice but if the mice take all our corn we will die! Save us, Great One! Help us, Great God!"

And a wind began to blow whoo-whoo-whooo. [much blowing!]

The wind blew harder ... whooo-whooooo.

And the sky grew daaaark!

And the wind blew harder ...

then there was the BIG sound of a thunder clap [my hand clap, followed by all the rest].

And another thunder clap [*improved synchronisation of the handclaps*].

And the lightning came down from the sky chkchkchk [*zig/zag hand movements*] [*and so on, for as long as I could stand it!*]

And the lightning, and the thunder, and the wind all made such a terrible noise that … a little mouse, every mouse, all the little mice ran down the corn, they were so afraid, they ran down the corn and on to the earth and off, off to the edge of the plain and into the forest and up, up, up into the Douglas pine trees and there they hid, up in the trees and they never went into the corn again. The corn was saved. The corn was saved at last from the teeth of the mice.

But let me tell you something. The mice were so afraid that they left the marks of where they had hidden themselves forever after. Look, I'll show you. Look at all these cones I've got. These are like the seeds of the pine trees. Cones. Look, I've got lots of different kinds here, see, big ones and little ones, tight ones like this and spready ones. All sorts.

But these are the special ones. This is a pine cone from a Douglas pine tree, the very trees which hid the mice. Where they left their mice marks.

Do you see? The mice hid themselves away from the thunder and the lightning inside the pine cones and there's where they hid — you see? — their little back legs and their tails hanging down. Forevermore.

Author's version

The Bald, Warty Giant

Once long ago there lived a terrible giant. He had no friends because everyone was afraid of him. He was even afraid of himself for one day he had looked into the crystal clear water of the lake and he had seen his own reflection.

Now he lived by himself in a cave on the side of a mountain.

"No wonder people are afraid of me," he thought. "I am so ugly." The giant had a huge bald head and warts all over his skin. "What can I do to make myself beautiful?" he thought.

Just then he heard a sound. It was the sound of laughter. The giant hid right at the back of the cave. After a few minutes he peeped out to see a beautiful little girl with golden hair. She was looking at herself in the water. "How I wish I looked like her," said the giant, "then everyone would like me."

Slowly, ever so slowly, he crept out of the cave. The little girl turned and saw him. "Don't be afraid, I won't harm you," said the giant.

The little girl laughed and said, "I'm not afraid. Everyone in the village said you were terrible but I had to come and see you for myself."

The giant found that he could talk to the little girl and he told her all about how he wished he did not frighten people.

"I will help you," said the girl. "In my village there are many beautiful birds with long, colourful tail feathers. If we collect the feathers that the birds shed then you can have a wig to wear."

The giant thought that was a good idea. The little girl took hold of the giant's hand and promised him she would be back the next day with some feathers.

When the little girl got home she told her friends all about the giant. They told her that they were too frightened to go up themselves but she promised them that when the giant looked beautiful they could play with him. So it was that all the children from the village set about collecting the long, colourful tail feathers from the beautiful birds, and the next day the little girl met the giant once more. She had all the feathers in a string bag and she had found some special glue in her father's shed. The giant was really pleased to see her.

Very carefully the little girl climbed on to the giant's shoulders and very gently she spread the special glue over his bald head. Then she quickly stuck the feathers into the glue before it dried. When she had finished, the giant looked at himself in the lake. He was very pleased with his new wig. "But what about my warts?" he said.

The little girl looked at him and said, "My mum has got some cream. I will bring it with me tomorrow."

The little girl hurried home and asked her mother if she could borrow the special cream from her dressing table and she explained to her mother why she needed it. Her mother thought she was being silly but she let her daughter put the cream into her bag for the next day.

As soon as it was daylight the little girl went to the giant's cave. She carefully put the cream onto the giant's face. It covered all his warts and spots. In fact the giant looked much better.

"Can my friends come and see you now?" asked the little girl. "Yes," said the giant. He liked his new face and hair very much indeed.

The little girl ran back to the village and brought all the children to the cave to see the giant. He came out of his cave and smiled to see all the children. They climbed and scampered all over his body and the giant loved to play with the children.

But as the days went by the feathers began to drop off the giant's head and the cream wore away to show his warts and spots. The giant grew ugly again and he crept back towards his cave.

"Where are you going?" cried the children.

"I am ugly. I don't want you to be frightened of me again," he said.

But the children said they had not noticed his ugliness. They loved him for what he was, a kind and gentle giant.

And the giant was never lonely again.

Chris Sterling

The Giant Injection

The dreaded day was approaching. When Mrs Bishop had given out the forms all those weeks ago the stories started immediately. It began with those who had older brothers and sisters. "Your arm goes dead for three days!" Michael Benton had told them, revelling in the imaginary pain. "My brother had to wear his arm in a sling."

"The actual needle is really thick and you need cotton wool to soak up the blood!" BLOOD! Somehow the word was more terrible than the fact (especially when it was Michael Benton saying it).

The worst moment of all in those days before the injection was when Sean Parkinson had told her about the little injection they gave you first so that they could deaden your arm a bit for the big one!

This worried Laura, particularly since Sean Parkinson was usually a reliable source of information, not given to gossip and not a boy who oozed when he said the word "blood".

Of course, none of the children dared share their fears with Mrs Bishop. She had given out the forms so efficiently, and crisply challenged the class with the words, "We're not going to have any nonsense from 1B are we?"

Everyone had done their best lying that morning, even Peter Beech who had cried and wet himself when, in vest and pants, they had lined up outside the sick room for their medicals last April.

By the time Laura was able to count how many days away the injection actually was she knew that it was really a darning needle attached to a litre pop bottle, made to look like something she remembered from a doctor's set she used to have.

Knowing that they kindly deadened your arm first was no consolation.

Confiding in dad the night before while they were doing the dishes together he had told her that Sean Parkinson had made up that part, that when he was at school ... Laura hadn't heard what happened when dad was at school. She knew he was just trying to make it easier for her and dad's words were drowned out by the imagined two-foot long syringe with a knitting needle on the end of it.

That Friday morning attempts to hide hysteria under the calm surface perceived by Mrs Bishop were failing. Peter Beech was missing for ten minutes and returned in his PE shorts. Michael Benton kept whispering "Blood blood" but still tried to get to the back of the queue.

Laura rolled up her left sleeve and waited. She'd decided she wouldn't even look at the first needle, just in case. She worked out how she could steer herself into the room, sort of backwards, without seeing anything. The teachers had been crafty as usual and had sent everyone through the sick room and out of the door at the other end. That was so you couldn't see all the blood on their arms, or ask anyone, "What was it like?"

It was Laura's turn. Walking in sideways she fixed her eyes on a poster about cleaning your teeth and, gritting hers, she waited for the first injection. A slight discomfort, a little pressure on the skin, a strange antiseptic coldness in her arm. Not too bad. But her arm certainly wasn't dead enough to encounter the giant injection without flinching. Should she tell them? Should she scream out, "It's not worked! I must have funny arms or something. You'd better not do it!" Just as she struggled with her instincts she heard the familiar voice of the school nurse, "Are you all right Laura? I said, that's fine, you can go now."

Laura was about to remind them that she hadn't had the second injection but, holding a small wad of cotton wool on an even smaller little pin prick on her arm, she decided instead that perhaps she wouldn't always take notice of Sean Parkinson.

Carol A Cooke

Chaim and the Chrane

There was once a little Jewish tailor called Chaim who lived in a house just behind the Philpot Street Synagogue. Suits and overcoats he could make like nobody else. But he fell on hard times. He wasn't the only one. The tailoring, everyone said, had one foot in the grave. Suits fit for a Rothschild gathered dust. Seeing his family suffering, he made up his mind to try something different to make ends meet. In the small yard at the back of his house nothing grew in the dusty black soil except some struggling weeds and a large patch of a tough plant with long coarse leaves. You wouldn't give it a second look but Chaim knew that it was from the roots of this plant that you could make chrane, horseradish sauce with beetroot. It had foot-long knobbly roots which you grated while the tears ran from your eyes. Every Friday before shabbas came in he had seen his wife Ruchele grate the chrane, tears running down her cheeks. With a little beetroot it would be ready for the shabbas chicken. So Chaim, knowing that shabbas without chrane is like pesach without matzos, set himself up a little business. The bespoke tailor became a bespoke chrane maker and he sold his little jars from an old pram on a corner in Wentworth Street. Do I need to tell you he didn't make a fortune, move to Golders Green, and make good marriages for his daughters? But he scraped a living.

Poor Chaim, he was soon in deep trouble again. He had used up every root in the yard. He watched his stock of jars dwindling to a dozen or so. There was nothing for it but to look for another source of supply. But what little East End tailor knew where to find chrane growing? Poor Chaim couldn't have told you where to find an oak tree or a dandelion. What should he do? Take a bus to Epping Forest and search for the long coarse leaves? He certainly hadn't seen any in Victoria Park. He was in despair until he remembered Mendele. If you believed the yuchnas in Hessel Street market you would believe that Mendele had once been a respected rabbi, but because he had dabbled in the cabbala and god knows what black arts, they threw him out. Still, Chaim thought to himself, a clever man is a clever man, a malamed is a malamed, even if he can't turn beigels into golden bracelets.

So Chaim took himself to Mendele's dark little room crammed with old books, sheets and sheets of notes scribbled in Hebrew with strange signs which Chaim had never seen before. When Mendele had let him in, he poured out his story. Mendele listened without saying a word.

He just sat there wrinkling up his leathery face, scratched behind his yamulka and twiddled his beard. "Chaim," he said, "I can tell you where to find this plant in abundance, as easily as I can tell you how to get from here to the shvitzig in Brick Lane."

"Tell, tell," said Chaim.

"There's more to it than that. Such good fortune doesn't drop in a man's way like manna. The manna days are over and done with. The Red Sea don't part for us any more."

Quaking, Chaim reached for his purse, knowing it was unlikely he could offer enough.

"Put it away, put it away," Mendele said irritably. "I will direct you to a place where you will find enough chrane to last you till the Messiah comes. You know the old Jewish burial ground? Alongside is a plot of waste ground. Go and look there. Only that waste ground must be treated with as much respect as the burial ground itself. Just remember one thing though," and he looked Chaim straight in the eye, "What will happen when you start rooting around I cannot say."

"What can happen?" Chaim's voice was a whisper. Mendele was already turning to his books. He behaved as if Chaim wasn't there. Not a word could be dragged from him. Chaim ran from the room, praying all the way home. He told Ruchele what Mendele had said.

"That meshigenah," she said, "You trust him? I've heard about him. His head is like an old booba's bag stuffed full of bits and pieces. All the same don't go up to the cemetery. The evil eye looks upon it. Old Chainik, may his soul rest in peace, once walked past there ..."

"Enough! Enough! said Chaim. "Make a couple of platzels with chopped herring or something, I'm going right now. I'll dig out as much as I can carry."

Ruchele, seeing there was no help for it, put up some lunch for him and he took a large sack and the fork he had used to dig his own chrane. A little anxious in heart, he set out for the old burial ground. As soon as he arrived, he rushed over to the waste ground. Sure enough there was clump after clump of sturdy horseradish plants. He threw down his lunch bag and straight away got on with the business of digging out the roots, thinking of all the of jars and jars of chrane ready for sale. After a while he began to slow down. It was almost more than he could carry. Ai, Mendele, he thought, they can say what they like but those books and that little head have worked a little miracle for me.

He suddenly felt hungry and sat down, opened his lunch bag and munched away on his chopped herring platzels. When he was eating he felt the sweat he had worked up go cold on him and he noticed a sharp wind was blowing through the old gravestones and bending the leaves of the horseradish. It was getting misty too. Then it grew darker, then darker until he found himself platzel in hand in pitch darkness. The wind grew ferocious and so powerful was it that he was suddenly whisked up into the air and twirled round and round, his arms and legs flailing about. He turned head over heels again and again. That Mendele and his cursed books, he kept thinking. May the cholera take him.

Soon he felt himself coming to earth and he landed gently as a feather from a passing bird. Relieved as he was to have come safely to earth, he was still dismayed to find himself in pitch darkness. But the cobbles of a road were under his feet and after a while he could see in the distance a bright light. Where there's light there's people, he thought. I'll get out of this schemozzle yet. So he stepped briskly along the street dimly aware of houses and shops on either side of him. Not a sound came from one of them, not a window or door was open. He pressed on until he came to the house where light was streaming through the open door. He could see, sitting one each side of a bright fire, an old man and an old woman. "Come in, come in," the woman said. "Take a chair to the fire and sit down. I'll get you a bite to eat." She set before him a plate of wurst, pickled cucumber, cold salt beef and black rye bread.

"May your children have good luck and grandchildren also," said Chaim, his mind still trying to catch up with events. They smiled and watched him eat.

When he had finished, the old man said, "It's too early for bed, so tell us a story."

"Me!" said Chaim. "I could make you a suit like you wouldn't find in Saville Row but tell a story, never. I've listened to Schmiel the Shikke tell hundreds when he's had one or two but I can't remember a single one. Bella with the egg stall can tell stories would make the eyes pop out of your head. But me ... no, I like to listen."

"Oh well," said the woman in a bit of a huff, "supper you can eat, your toes you can toast in front of the fire but a story you can't manage. Maybe, Mr Gentleman, you could manage to fetch in a bucket of coal from the shed in the backyard."

Chaim was only too willing. He picked up the coal bucket, went out to the shed, filled the bucket with coal, stood it down and paused for breath. As he did so, once again he was swept off his feet, whisked into the air and buffeted about. He turned over and over, half falling, half floating. He landed lightly in pitch darkness. In the darkness he saw a bright light, much brighter than the first time. "Where there's light ..." he said to himself.

Once again he headed down a street in which every house was dark, bolted and barred. He arrived at the open door of a big house. From inside he could hear the sound of a baby crying and a babble of excited voices. He walked into a large room and he could tell in a moment from the table full of food and the way the men had grouped themselves around the baby that any minute there was going to be a circumcision. And then he noticed, among the women seated in a huddle at the far end of the room, a beautiful dark-haired young woman who beckoned to him and had him stand beside her. At that very moment a big fellow with a black beard shouted out, "The moel is ten minutes late already. A disgrace. Maybe we could get old Gottlieb."

Just as someone made for the door the beautiful girl at Chaim's side stepped forward and said, "No need. Chaim here is the best moel from Stamford Hill to Whitechapel." She have him a little push.

"Me!" said Chaim, "Are you meshiggah? I would do the little baby a terrible injury. God forbid. Me with a surgeon's knife! I wouldn't trust myself to bandage a cut finger. Anyway I can't stand the sight of blood. What sort of mishegas is this?"

The young woman said in his ear sharply, "Don't make me a liar in front of all these people."

Suddenly Chaim found himself in the moel's garments, a scalpel in his hand. Without a moment's hesitation he stepped forward and deftly removed the baby's foreskin. As is the custom the baby screamed its head off. "Shush tatele," said the baby's father, well satisfied that the deed was at last done.

"Now," said the big man with the beard, "if we had someone who could play the fiddle. A briss without music who ever heard of such a thing? Such a pity."

The beautiful woman next to Chaim spoke up again. "Don't worry, don't worry. Chaim here can play like Heifetz. He'll have you tapping your feet and dancing in no time."

"Fiddler!" said Chaim, "A nice bit of fiddling is a blessing but if I scraped a fiddle you'd all go running out of the room. To me a fiddler is a miracle."

"A little joke," said the woman. "He loves a little joke." Turning to Chaim she whispered, "So you want to make me an idiot in front of all the guests."

In a flash Chaim was standing there fiddle and bow at the ready. "It's true," someone said, "Like Heifetz. Such a fiddler you don't hear at every briss."

The big man called for silence. "You know," he said, "if Itzig's son, Avrum — the one with all those degrees — were here, we would have a lovely speech. Like to finish things off. Such a pity."

"A speech," said the woman. "You think we won't have a speech when we have here Chaim, the best speechmaker in the whole community."

Chaim mumbled and muttered. "Speeches yet. Anyone who knows me will tell you I wouldn't say boo to a goose. They say I'm like Bontshe Schweig in the story, a man of very few words. If I start talking in company, my throat goes dry. I try to say something and words don't come out."

"Such modesty you only find in great men," said the woman to the guests. In Chaim's ear she said, 'How will I hold my head up again? Mrs Stein would give an arm and a leg to see me made such a fool."

Chaim climbed on a chair and was soon delivering a speech full of jokes and witticisms and some philosophising about life which everyone liked because it was a bit over their heads. When he started quoting Maimonides they glowed. "Ach, such a speech you only hear once in a lifetime."

It seemed to Chaim that the room had become unbearably stuffy. He went to stand in the doorway for a breath of fresh air. As he stood there that strange sensation came on again and he was once more snatched into the air and flung hither and thither. This time when he landed he found himself back at the shed with the bucket of coal in front of him. Though he was a bit confused at first, he soon gathered his wits, picked up the bucket of coal and went back into the house. The old couple were sitting by the fire exactly as he had left them. He put the bucket on the hearth and drew a chair up to the fire. After a few moments' silence the old man said, "Soon time for bed. So tell us Chaim, can you tell us a story?"

"Oy have I got a story, have I got a story," said Chaim and he told them everything which had happened since he went out to get coal.
"A story is like good luck," said the old woman. "Now wherever you go, if someone asks for a story, they'll know you're a storyteller for sure."

They had a supper that night like it was a festival — chicken soup with kneidlech, liver rissoles with latkes and sweet honig lekach to finish up with. They put Chaim in a feather bed and he slept and slept. He dreamt that a big man with a beard was buying one of his bespoke suits and stroking it like it was a precious fur. When he woke up he wasn't in the feather bed anymore but in the waste ground next to the graveyard. By his side was his lunch bag, his digging fork and the sackful of horseradish roots. He picked them up and headed for Ruchele and home.

And I can tell you, he hasn't needed to fill another jar with chrane from that day to this, by my life so sure.

Harold Rosen

I Remember Ponty

We caught a little fat James bus to it or a double decker United Welsh, which ran along the main road from Swansea to Ystradgynlais, getting on at the Mond stop in Clydach where I lived out my childhood and adolescence ... three miles from Clydach it was; nine miles from Swansea. That was the only road to Pontardawe for regular traffic, running alongside the Tawe river and the canal.

Footsloggers could get to Ponty along the canal tow path. I walked that with my mother when I was little ... with others later. She would pick me up from Clydach Junior School armed with her shopping basket containing cheese sandwiches, a couple of russet apples, a bottle of pop and a paper bag full of her fairy cakes each topped with a bit of glacé cherry. We'd sit and eat our picnic on a patch of grassy bank where there were kingcups growing — mollyblobs my mother called them but others say mayblobs or mareblobs or marybuds or, if you really enjoy learning names, *caltha palustris*. Mollyblobs to us, out of sight of any skeletal pram or bogey cart or rusty bike which sometimes pokes out of the mustardy canal waters.

When we got to Ponty we'd go to the pictures. At first it was Pinocchio or the Three Stooges or Old Mother Riley and her daughter Kitty or Laurel and Hardy. By the time I reached my term in the top class, before I took the Scholarship to the grammar school and after the measles, chicken pox and German measles, we absorbed musical films together. There was *Annie Get Your Gun*, *Seven Brides for Seven Brothers*, *Oaklahoma*, *Brigadoon*, *Carousel* and other such lilting roundabouts, wondrous whirligigs to relish inside my singing head afterwards. Singing, singing inside all the way to the lit-up bus stop on the main road by the traffic lights and below the dark wood that climbed up the the slopes of Mynydd Gellionen opposite. How I wished my mother would stop her jovial nattering at me! All I wanted was to be Doris Day in private with Howard Keel, making romantic music.

There was only one other route to Pontardawe and that was the mountain way which was not exactly a road — it couldn't have been else my father would not have given me my first driving lessons on it: there were no L plates on the family Hillman, just KG 8875 which to this day is the only car registration number I can instantly quote. No, the mountain road was just a track, really. Mynydd Gellionen wasn't exactly a mountain either, being just short of 1000 feet high as my father frequently and scornfully pointed out. But just as kingcups remain mollyblobs, hills like that remain mountains to me even now especially in rolling Wiltshire which my husband and I visit quite frequently. The past is always with you.

You couldn't see the valley road, the river or the canal from the plateau top of Mynydd Gellionen nor could they see you because of the trees on the Ponty edge of it. By the time my taste in words and song had moved out of American celluloid musicals and into verse and madrigal, I used to go up there as often as I could, by myself mainly. Halfway up, well beyond the municipal houses where there was nothing but countryside, I'd crouch under a milk churn stand out of the wind and strike matches on the dry-stone wall to light up the Du Maurier I'd sneaked out of my mother's everlasting packet. She hardly smoked at all. She didn't inhale the way my sister had taught me to do but would puff nervously at an occasional cigarette every few days, very boring.

Once atop, there were undulating stretches upon stretches of wiry grass which was a bit greyish because, my father said, of pollution caused by the smoke from the Mond Nickel works in Clydach. But the grass looked good enough to me. And so did the slopes and the curves and the boggy flats and the ferns and the scrunchy round clumps of shrubby leaves with juicy berries under. And there was so much sky up above. I could forget my theft of nicotine along with all my other sins and indulge in rich religious pantheistic sensations. Spiritual feeling may have been assisted by the presence of the 'five mile' chapel which stood in the middle of this nowhere in defiance of the English overlord who had once imposed a specific legal measure between the sitings of chapels to make life difficult for heathen non-conformity. Once a year we had a Sunday School picnic among its gravestones from the Wesleyan Methodist chapel (no relation to the chapel on the mountain — Welsh Methodists were Calvinistic) in the village.

Years later, I treasured rather more ecstatic moments in the same spot with Tudor Williams, my first love, *Bassanio mio*, under the skylarks and the setting summer sun, lips purple from the bilberies — or wimberries or myrtleberries or blaeberries or whortleberries or *vacciniun myrtillus berries* ... what did a name signify at such a time

> When the sweet wind did gently kiss the trees
> And they did make no noise ...

as Lorenzo did say?

I'd waited long enough for such a time, god knows. Beautiful Tudor! I'd loved him ever since Miss David chose me from the fourth year to be Portia with all the fifths and sixths, including Tudor as Bassanio. There were five public performances in all, drawing the crowds from Pontardawe, Clydach, Ystalyfera, Ystradgynlais, Rhiwfawr, Rhydyfro, Cwmllynfell, Godregraig, Cwmtwrch, Graigcefnpark, Brynamman, Gwauncaegurwen and all the rest of the unlikely world for all I cared. What mattered to me was ... a kiss when Bassanio chose the right casket, a kiss when we met in Act V, equals two kisses per night; five performances equals ten kisses total in one week: bliss! I waited a whole year for some more where they came from, with only the mountain sheep to see!

I don't remember how I won him but I lost him on account of Ponty Rink. The Rink was the mecca of all senior secondary school pupils thereabouts. It may have been a skating rink once but at that time it was widely famed among the young, and notorious among the old, as the valley dance hall. Anyone with any spunk went to the Rink on a Saturday night — where else? My father banned it from his own family so I only know of it in wishful thinking but my sister got there more than once because she was brave. I never once went to the Rink. My father convinced me it was a place of smoke, drunkenness and other unspecified depravities. Tudor, the love of my life, went every week but I refused to compromise in the matter even when I was 'going with' him. 'Going with' Tudor meant supporting his rugby playing on Saturday afternoons and accompanying him up Mynydd Gellionen on Sunday evenings. That lasted until I discovered he had been dancing with Bethan Davies inside the rink when I thought he was spending the night with his Auntie Megan in Tonypandy. He also invited her for a walk along the canal bank during the evening and escorted her all the way home after. Two-timing me he was, so I spurned him, love or no love, and never again cast an eye upon the agile outside-half of the All Whites.

At the negative end of the entertainment spectrum from the Cinema and the Rink was Pontardawe Grammar School. My sister had been a pupil there but I was obliged to go further up the valley to Ystalyfera Grammar because my sister had got up to such larks at Ponty that my father felt I should be allowed an unblemished start where the family escutcheon was unknown. Sometimes I went to Ponty school to see their school plays. I saw *Androcles and the Lion,* there. I saw Sian Phillips in *Tobias and the Angel* long, long before she became famous and married Peter O'Toole. That is, I saw most of *Tobias and the Angel;* I missed the last portion because I'd arranged to meet Islwyn, Tudor's successor, down the hill from the school at the not-so-well lit bus stop, by the bus station. Islwyn was a pupil at Pontardawe Grammar. He was tall, blonde, elegant, smooth cheeked and faintly sweet smelling, like Johnson's baby powder. There was a lot to be said for a stroll with him down by the canal in the dark as long as I got a bus to get me home — from the play — by ten.

When I arrived at the bus stop he was not there. No one was as far as I could see. It was very spooky all alone beside shuttered shops and the great gaping cavern of the bus station, while everyone else was watching Sian Phillips being an angel.

From the shadowy doorway of the sweetshop came a deep, dark voice. "Left early, h'an't yer?"

I turned in fear, and glimpsed a bulky masculine shape sway slightly in the darkest corner. I did what I always had planned to do if an evil stranger accosted me which was to invent an imminent protector. "I'm waiting ..." (voice unnaturally high pitched and unfamiliar) "... I'm waiting for my brother!"

In that same instant I spotted Islwyn's blond head, gleaming white a hundred yards off as he passed under the nearest street lamp and simultaneously, too, realised the identity of the evil stranger. He taught history at Ponty Grammar and had recently married Miss David, English teacher, producer of *The Merchant of Venice* and provider of tickets for Ponty School's rendering of *Tobias and the Angel*. Miss David, Miss David's mother, and Miss David's new husband all knew my mother and they all knew she had two daughters and no sons.

Next day, Miss David (as we continued to call her in spite of the rival school's Head of History) fixed me with her evil eye in the corridor. "Oh, Betty," she leered with many teeth. "And how's ..." big pause, "your ..." even bigger pause, "brother?"

I tried to explain but it sounded to both of us like a pack of lies. Teachers can so easily rob you of your language.

After the phone call from Sandra Temple I looked up Pontardawe in our RAC Handbook, 1967-68 edition which we've never replaced. It wasn't there. I looked up Clydach. That was in with a few boring facts plus, incredibly, the words *Golf, Pontardawe, 10 holes*. So, according to the RAC, Pontardawe's only claim to fame was its provision of a golf course for those with a traveller's interest in Clydach. The Ponty I knew had a main road, canal bank path and a mountain track leading to it from Clydach; a cinema; a Rink; and a Grammar School. Houses and a few shops, of course ... but I'd never heard of any golf course. I couldn't imagine anyone from the valley playing golf. It must have been there for the management and foreign friends of the Mond Nickel. I decided to ask Sandra about the golf course when I went to give that talk.

Autobiographical

Usheen

I want to tell you about the land of the Ever Young. And about Usheen, one of the last of the great Irish warriors, who went there and came away again.

Now Usheen was a fine young man, tall, with long black silken hair, raven black, and his eyes as blue as the bluest, stillest, sunniest sea. Blue they were, as Galway bay itself when no clouds float over it. And there were no clouds upon Usheen's brow for laughter was there upon his lips and in the corners of his eyes.

Usheen would go hunting with his brothers and with others too. And on this day when he and his brothers were riding their horses through the forest a great stag emerged out of the undergrowth and leapt up before them. A fine beast he was and the hooves of the horses thundered as after it they went, the hounds baying, but the stag was too swift for the whole pack of them. Its feet were crackling the twigs beneath and its antlers clacking amongst the branches overhead. It raced them all, twining in and out amongst the trees of the forest, round about, in and out, and trouble it was indeed to keep him in sight. Finally the beast made for the sea and leapt into it with a great sploosh! He swam out, he swam deep. Down he went until only the tips of his antlers pricked the surface of the waters.

Now, about two hundred yards from the shore there was a single rock which spiked out of the sea and the stag pulled his way up on to that rock and poised his feet on the very pinnacle of it. He stood there and stared at the hunters who did not follow him. He stared and stared, right into the deep blue eyes of Usheen, the brave. The beast would not be coming back so that day's hunting was done and the brothers returned home.

The very next day the warriors went out again on their fine horses, hoping for better success. Yet again the stag appeared before them. They chased it and they chased it but still it was beyond them. Again it reached the rocky shore, plunged into the waves and the same thing happened as on the day before. Up upon the rock it went and stared from its perch into, it seemed, the eyes of Usheen alone. And the hunters did not follow.

Usheen and his brothers decided they would go hunting once more

171

but this time they would cheat the stag of his escape. One of them would swim out to that rock and when the stag came there the warrior would grasp the stag and keep it. So they drew lots and it fell to Usheen himself to wait at the rock for the quarry. And that he did, silently, with only the soft lapping of the waves for company. Meanwhile the huntsmen set off into the grey forest and sure enough, just as before, the stag came out and he led them a merry dance, he did, and the twigs lashed the huntsmen's cheeks in the chase. But in the finish, as before, he went towards the sea and into the very sea itself, disappearing out of sight for long moments. He scrambled his way up the rock — but this time Usheen was there. Usheen grabbed him by the antlers. The great beast tossed Usheen right across his broad wet back and, with Usheen upon him and with Usheen's hands grasped tightly round his antlers, the creature hurled himself back into the waters and neither was seen again.

The stag took Usheen down, down to that enchanted land of no Time at all, the land of Tir-Nan-Oge. Indeed a timeless place it is, where twenty years can pass but will seem like half an hour. And if you were to seek it out, sure they say you would have to travel to the other side of the earth and find the very end of the world before you'd reach Tir-Nan-Oge. And this, they say, would take you one hundred years and a day — too long, too late, too old you would then be to dwell in the land of the Ever Young. And yet ... and yet there are those who say that Tir-Nan-Oge is not there at all but in this place, in the here and now, where you are and I am, in every place. Perhaps it is, perhaps, for some, maybe.

Everything is good in Tir-Nan-Oge, a place of beauty, all the beauties of heaven are there. And Usheen was glad to be where the stag had taken him and he did not feel the years slip by. But the moment came when Usheen said to himself, "Would that I could see my brothers again and the fine young men who went hunting with me." And he went to the Powers that Be in Tir-Nan-Oge and told them what he wanted.

"Your brothers are dead and gone long since," they said.

Now Usheen knew that was not true, for so little time had passed. It seemed to him that his journeying behind the antlers of the great stag was but a twelve month gone. "I will go," said Usheen, the warrior.

"Very well," they said, "Go if you must." And they put him on a white horse. "Go and see for yourself, then, but do not get off the horse or touch the earth of the old country."

And they put Usheen and his horse down in his own land and the warrior rode and rode until he came to the place where he was born. He looked around him for his brothers and his friends but every face he saw was the face of a stranger. For sure, his brothers, his family, his friends had died many, many years before.

He went to the place where his house had been. It was no longer there — just boulders and rubble clothed in moss and lichens and hanging ivy. Then what did he see beyond, untouched by time, just as it had always been, but a stone trough with clear crystal water in it. It was from that trough that they would drink the sweet water to slake their thirst. It was there they refreshed themselves in the morning and in the evening they would cup their hands in it and throw it over themselves, splashing away the sweat of the day. And cool water it was. It twinkled and winked at him now and he had a great feeling for it and a desire to drink there.

He forgot the warning he had been given by the Powers of Tir-Nan-Oge. He jumped off the horse. As soon as his feet touched the ground all the years that had passed came upon him and he shrank and shrivelled into an old man, and fell to the earth, a senseless thing, and all life left him.

Author's version

The Fisherman and the Mermaid

Once there was a fisherman, and lonely he was as he sat by himself of an evening in front of the turf burning in his fireplace. Now the fishermen in those parts of the northwest coast of Ireland lived with their families in little whitewashed cottages, under their cosy roofs which were thatched with straw and grasses. But the fisherman of my story, he had no wife and he had no children to keep him company at his own hearth. Sometimes when he could bear his silent home no longer, he'd climb his way down to the sand and the sea wrack at the bottom of the cliffs. Up and down, up and down the beach he'd pace while the moonlight glistened on the curled waves. In that place full of sea and sky with a backcloth of mountains beyond, the poor fisherman felt small and unloved.

"Sure, if I had a wife of my own like other men, I'd love her and cherish her to my dyin' day, that I would," he would say to himself, and sigh.

Sometimes people would gather in one another's houses of an evening to share stories, stories much like the one I'm telling you now. The other fishermen would tell him where the meeting was to be.

"Don't be such an aegit," they would say, "sittin' all by yourself in your own place when there are people to meet and tales to be told! Get yourself up, man, and be doin'."

But the fisherman could take neither the hustle and bustle of the gathering together nor the communal hush that settled around the voice of the storyteller, for when all was done his own cottage seemed afterwards as empty as death to him. Many a time he'd set out with good intent, but if the moon were bright and the tide had not yet reached up to base of the cliffs, his feet would take him not to the ceilidh but across the field and down the winding path in the cliff side to the deserted beach. Up and down, up and down he would walk alone, seeking solace in the swoosh, swoosh of the waves pulling and pushing at the gravelly sand.

And so it was on this night that I'm telling you. All alone in the fulness of the moon the fisherman was walking on the shore when suddenly he heard a strange and beautiful sound. It was a voice, a woman's voice, singing. The notes came from the north end of the beach, where the rocks huddled together. A sweet, high-pitched sound it was, slow and melancholy, and it drew the fisherman along and along to the end of the sand, up to the rocks and he squeezed his way through between two big rocks and came out on the other side, so he did.

And would you believe, on a flat rock in front of him, with her back towards him, singing and combing her long black hair, wasn't there a mermaid sitting? And behind her, plain to be seen spread out in the moonlight, wasn't there the mermaid's magic garment?

Now it's a known fact that a mermaid cannot enter the water without the wearing of her magic garment. And if anyone steals the mermaid's magic garment, sure she is in thrall to the thief, and must follow him wherever he may lead her, even to the very ends of the earth.

So the fisherman tiptoed over the rock and, light as a feather, he gathered up the mermaid's magic garment, rolled it small and thrust it into his pocket. And just as quick he turned away through the two big rocks and back along the beach he walked, back the way he had come and he did not stop, he did not stop, not even when the singing stopped but on and on he walked and he did not look behind him until he reached the little path that lead up the side of the cliff, then and only then he stopped and looked over his shoulder.

And there she was. Standing upon the sand, beside the rocks. Gazing after him.

"It's follow me you must, my lady, whether you will or no," said the fisherman to himself, and he made his way up the cliff, over the fields, through his garden gate, up the path, into his own kitchen and it was then, and not until then, that out of his pocket he took the magic garment. And he let it hang, like a wee hammock, between his two cupped hands. He looked at it for a good long while. What beautiful cloth it was, and that's the truth, with the moonlight shining through the open doorway upon it, the colours merging and twining together — blues of the sea and the sky, greens of the sea weed and the sedge grass, and the brown of the wet shore sand. The fisherman gazed in wonder at it, so he did, when suddenly a shadow fell across the gossamer threads that rested upon his fingers. He looked up.

There she was, the mermaid herself, still as stone in the doorway. Her eyes were wide and staring, for wasn't it the first time she had ever stood with a thatched roof above her head and stone flags beneath her feet? Wasn't it the first time she'd seen a warm hearth, or peat burning in a grate — strange indeed, for there is no fire under the ocean's ceiling? While she stood, mesmerised, hypnotised, the fisherman slipped out past her, out of the cottage and, in a flash, had the magic garment hidden away out of sight in the best place he could think of, which was underneath the thatch beside one of the doorposts. There it would stay dry and safe.

The mermaid's bewildered gaze fell upon him when he re-entered the kitchen. "Oh where is my magic garment?" she said.

"It's safe enough where it is," said he, "as safe as if it were on your back under the ocean."

"If ever I find my garment again, it's back to the water I shall go," said the mermaid.

"I daresay you would," replied the fisherman, "if that day should ever come, but perhaps it won't. Perhaps you'll find a better life with the feel of the earth about your feet and the love of a man to shelter you from harm."

Now the mermaid stayed there that night and the next night too, and the next. And the fisherman got land clothes for her. And in due time, they were married in the little church on the hill, just like other fishermen had been and would be again throughout the centuries to come.

As the weeks went by the little mermaid learned to love her husband for he thought nothing too good for his watery bride and he tried every way he could to bring smiles to her lips. Their love grew with each week and month and year that passed and by the time the seventh year had come and gone three children had been born to the couple, two girls and a boy. Such joy there was amongst them all that the fisherman forgot that his wife was a creature of the sea who once had a magic garment to wrap herself in.

But how could the mermaid forget? How could she stop her thoughts from journeying back to the place from whence she had come? How can anyone forget the earliest days, the beginnings of things?

Sometimes when she stood at the kitchen table kneading dough or rolling pastry, the turf fire would be hot on her back and how she would long for cool salt waters to swaddle her. And in the evenings, chatting together the two of them when the children were in their beds, sure the smoke of the fire and the smoke of the fisherman's pipe would wind its way into her nostrils and she would sigh for the clean smell of the sea spray. And at night as she lay staring at the moonlit walls of her bedroom, she would watch the shadows of the curtains move this way and that in the breeze from the open window, and she was reminded of the sea weed's graceful sway. She would lie still, listening for the seagull's cry and the soft slapping of the waves at the bottom of the cliffs. Though she loved her husband and her children dearly, the mermaid often paused to wonder where her magic garment could possibly be.

Now one day the fisherman decided to spruce up the little cottage and he gave it a good fresh coat of whitewash. But as for the thatch, well, it was all uneven and there was moss growing here and weeds growing there — one taller than the chimney even. It was time to get the thatcher. When the thatcher came he set out his tools, placed his ladder against the wall of the cottage and began his first task which was to get rid of the old thatch. Soon the air was full of dust and straw tossed hither and thither by the thatcher's pitchfork. Suddenly what came fluttering down with all the dirt and debris but the mermaid's magic garment! At that very moment the fisherman was looking out of the window and, with a gasp he leapt out of the door, picked it up off the path where it had settled and, for the second time in his life, he thrust the garment into his pocket. Round the back of the house he went to the corn stacks, all neatly piled for the new roof, and he thrust the garment between the sheaves. "That will be a safe spot for the moment," he said to himself, much relieved and a big sigh he sighed at the terrible thought of losing his wonderful wife, the mother of their children.

But you see now, he didn't know that the youngest of them, the wee boy, had been playing in the field watching the thatcher doing his work, and thinking to himself, "Maybe I won't be a fisherman like me dad when I grow to be a man. Maybe I'll be a thatcher instead, tossin' away the old like that and building the new." And then he saw it all, don't you see, the whole performance from beginning to end. He had crept round on the other side of the house to see what his father was doing with the beautiful cloth!

That night, after she'd given her son his nightly wash in the little tin bath in front of the kitchen fire and they were all alone and she was rubbing him dry on her knee in a big white towel, the child told his mother everything that he had seen as a small child would. "Sure a beautiful cloth it was, mother, all lovely colours of water and air and sand and things that grow in them, all woven together!"

And the mermaid's heart leapt up within her, and her salt-sea blood rushed in her veins. "I will go," she told herself, "and I shall be as I once was!"

That night she waited and waited until it was time for bed. She lay beside her dear husband, her eyes staring wide at the ceiling, her ears listening for her husband's breathing to turn into little snuffling snores. Then sleek as a fish she flowed out of her bed, down the wooden stairs and out of the back door. In the light of the moon the sheaves shone silvery stiff as the mermaid felt about amongst them. Soon her hand touched her own magic garment. She drew it out gently and pressed it to her breast for a wee while — then she was off and away, up the path, through the gate, across the fields, down the cliff path, and along the sand she flew to the north end of the beach where all the rocks were. And didn't she flit between the two big rocks to the very spot where the fisherman had seen her first?

And the mermaid takes and shakes her magic garment so the wind billows it like the sail of a ship, then she draws it to her pale self again, stepping into it and winding it round and round about her until she stands, her arms stretched to the moon above with the magic garment like a new skin upon her. Then she leapt into the water. In and out of the waves, over and under, singing as she went further and further out to sea, laughing and singing, diving and leaping, until she was no bigger than the head of a seal in the distance.

And she was gone.

And gone would be my story too, but that they say in those parts that sometimes, when the moon is full, the fisherman — who never ever stopped grieving and searching for his lost wife — would find high heaps of fish left on the flat rock for him by the mermaid. Certainly, there is no other way they could have got there. Sometimes he was sure he could hear her singing — but he never once glimpsed where she was.

And I'll tell you something more. Every now and then, so they say, there could be seen little wet footprints on the flagstones of the cottage floor, leading up the wooden stairs to the door of the children's bedroom. They say she would return to kiss her children's cheeks while they slept and she would gently comb their hair with a comb made of mother-of-pearl.

Author's version

The Fisherman and the Mermaid

Ailsa was a young girl you would surely notice in a crowd with her curly red hair and sea-green eyes. She lived, many years ago, with her mother and father, in a small house in a big city.

One summer, the weather was very much warmer than usual. The grass in the park was dried up and grey. The flowers made you want to sneeze; the hedges were dusty and the pavements felt gritty. Ailsa went to the local baths to cool down, but there wasn't enough room to swim without bumping into someone. She walked the long road to the library, but there weren't any good stories left.

One night, Ailsa lay on her bed, too hot to bear the blankets. She felt wideawake, so she climbed on a chair and opened the window. The cool night air touched her cheek, the moon shone brighter than the street lights and she heard a ship's hooter far off. She thought of the deep cool ocean, many miles away. The waves would be crashing against the rocks and the smooth sand and the little pebbles would feel damp under your bare feet where the waves crept up and slid back again.

Next morning, as if in answer to her dreamy thoughts, Ailsa's mother said, "We'll have to get packed up today because we're going to Grandpa's tomorrow, you know. The train leaves at nine in the morning."

The train journey was long and the sun dazzled through the windows of the carriage. Suddenly, Dad got up and let down the window in the carriage door. "Who can see the sea?" he asked. Ailsa concentrated. "There it is — I can see it," she said, pointing. She was always the first to detect the darker line of blue that came between the earth and the sky. Dad said he didn't believe her, but when the red and white sails of the little boats in the harbour appeared, he had to admit that she was right.

Grandpa had once been a fisherman, so his cottage was close to the beach. It was small and painted white with a low thatched roof and a tiny garden where Grandpa grew his vegetables and a few flowers. He lived alone with an old cat for company. Ailsa loved Grandpa. He had so many stories to tell about his days as a fisherman. He had nearly drowned once when his boat capsized in rough water in the middle of the Irish Sea. He knew stories, too, about wrecked ships he had seen under the water when he went diving as a boy.

Mum and Dad had often asked Grandpa to come to the city to stay with them. They worried about him living alone, now that he was old. But he said he was never lonely. Then, he would laugh and say that he wouldn't, in any case, be able to sleep without the sound of the waves to rock him off at night. Ailsa understood what he meant.

This year Ailsa went climbing with Dad on the rocks and he showed her all the best places to swim and to dive that he remembered from when he was a boy. They had picnics on the beach every day, played in the rock pools and collected seaweeds and shells to take home. The only thing that spoiled the holiday was that Grandpa refused to go down onto the beach with them.

"But why not?" Ailsa asked.

"No, I've got a bone in me leg today," he would laugh.

Or, "I can't. I've got to see a man about a dog."

Or, "Who'll make the tea if I'm out gallivanting?"

Ailsa wondered why Grandpa made so many excuses.

One morning, Ailsa woke up early, as usual. The seagulls were already screaming over the rocks and the waves were murmuring far out in the bay. "Low tide," she thought. She dressed and ran downstairs, expecting to find Grandpa, as usual, down before her, making a cup of tea or sitting in the sun smoking his pipe and nursing the cat.

Grandpa wasn't in the kitchen. He wasn't outside on the stone bench, not in the garden at the back. "He must have gone to the village," Ailsa thought, looking out of the front gate and up the road. But there was no sign of him. She decided to go down to the beach and see if there were any more good shells to add to her collection. Taking her small rucksack, she ran across the green in front of the cottage and then picked her way carefully down the steep path which led to the beach. She needed both hands to help herself down. She came to a point where you had to squeeze between two huge rocks; Ailsa always thought of this as the gateway to beach. Once through, she looked up and was startled to see Grandpa sitting with his back to her on the big flat picnic rock, looking out towards the sea. He didn't look round; he couldn't have heard her. She decided to creep up on him, give him a surprise.

She pulled herself up on the rock and crawled over, right up to Grandpa. He did not move. Then she put her hand on his shoulder and said, "Got you!" Grandpa gave a great shudder and slowly turned to look at her. His eyes were brimming with tears; he blinked and the tears began to run down his cheeks. Ailsa was shocked, for she had never seen Grandpa cry before.

"What's wrong, Grandpa? Have you hurt yourself? Did you fall down?"

Grandpa smiled very sadly and put his arm around Ailsa. "No, love, no," he said gently.

"What's the matter then?"

"I'm just thinking of the old times."

"What makes you so sad, though?"

Grandpa took a big white hankie out of his pocket and wiped his eyes, then blew his nose. "I'm thinking about your Granny. It's a long time since she was here with me. Your Dad was only a little lad then. It was hard for him without her."

"What happened to her?" Ailsa asked.

"It's a long story, a long story," he repeated.

"Tell me the story. I want to hear the story," Ailsa insisted.

Grandpa looked straight into her sea-green eyes. "I wonder," he muttered, "I wonder if I can."

"Yes — go on, Grandpa. I'm listening."

"Well, I have always lived in this cottage, you know. It belonged to my parents so I grew up here. They both died quite young, my Mum and Dad. My sisters got married and my brothers moved away to find work so I stayed on, alone. I had the boat and I'd always liked the fishing more than the others. I didn't see many people, only the lady at the post office when I went to get my shopping and a few men I drank with after selling my fish. Most of the time I'd be out laying my nets or bringing home the catch I didn't have a girlfriend and I was often quite lonely, especially on long winter evenings or when the sea was too rough to fish ..."

"How did you meet Granny, then?" Ailsa interrupted.

"Do you want the true story?"

"Yes."

"Well," — Grandpa looked at his pipe then out to sea again — "it was one night in summer. A brilliant moonlit night. I came down here to the beach; my heart was empty and I felt very sad and lonely. I came down that little path and squeezed through the gap just as you did today and then, just as I came up to this flat rock where we are sitting now, I saw her."

"Granny?" Ailsa asked in a whisper.

"I saw a mermaid, sitting with her back to me, combing her long red curls with a beautiful comb of mother-of-pearl. On the rock beside her was her mermaid's garment. It was a marvellous thing. It was blue like the blue of the sea, green like the green of the seaweed and gold like the gold of the sand of the shore. It was all shining in the moonlight.

"Now, I knew that mermaids change into human shape when they come on to dry land and that they cannot regain their mermaid-tails without their magic garments."

Ailsa stared at her Grandpa, her eyes full of questions.

"So, I reached out my hand and took the garment. It was silky to the touch and slipped through my fingers like water. As I hesitated there on the rock, with the garment already in my trouser pocket, she turned round. Her sea-green eyes looked long into mine and I fell in love with her. I knew at once that I wanted her to come to live with me in the cottage and be my wife."

"Did she say yes?" asked Ailsa.

"Later. But I didn't stop to ask at first. I left my coat on the rock and took her magic garment with me. I came back between the big rocks and up the path, always hoping that she would follow me but not daring to look behind. When I got the door and turned, she was right behind me with my coat around her shoulders. I built up the fire and invited her to sit on the settle beside it.

"As she did and as she warmed herself by the flames, I went out the back and found a place in the thatch where I could hide the magic sea-garment. I tucked it up, well out of sight.

"In due time, she came to love me. I called her Eilidh and we were married in the church in the village and, as you know, we had three children, Ina, Morag, and Alastair ..."

"Dad!" said Ailsa.

"Yes," Grandpa replies. "I was very happy for a long time and I forgot all about the magic sea-garment stuffed into the thatch."

"Was Granny Eilidh happy too?" Ailsa asked.

"I thought she was. She was a wonderful wife. She kept the house spotless. She was always washing the floor or cleaning the windows until they shone. She baked our bread and cooked our meals and she was a perfect mother. She really loved those children."

"Did she forget about the mermaid garment?"

"I thought she had." Grandpa pulled his collar up around his neck, although the sun was very warm by now.

"So ... what happened? Did she die, Grandpa?" Ailsa asked this question in a quiet gentle voice, her eyes anxiously scanning Grandpa's face.

He went on: "One spring when the flowers were all coming out in the garden, I thought the cottage needed to be freshened up, so I white-washed the walls, inside and out. Eilidh was pleased.

"As I painted I saw how the winter storms, the birds and perhaps mice had damaged the thatch. We decided, as the fish were selling well that year, we would get the thatcher to renew the roof that summer.

"He came over — Alex Gray it was from the village — and he worked a whole week on that roof. He took all the old straw off and piled it up in the yard behind the cottage.

"I remember how your Daddy watched Alex as he worked and wanted to help him, though he was only a little lad at the time. He loved his mother and used to tell her everything, as little boys will. I think it must have been him that told, yes, it must have been him ..."

"What did he tell, Grandpa?" Ailsa asked. "What happened?"

"The garment, as I told you, was in the thatch. Your Daddy must have seen it, seen it, lying, no doubt gleaming, in the pile of straw. Perhaps he took it to his mother or told her what he'd seen. It's the kind of thing he would have done then, you see, being little."

"Was she pleased to have it back?"

"That I can't say. She didn't talk to me about it. I think she must have been."

Grandpa looked out to sea and his eyes filled with tears again. "She left us that night and I never saw her again."

"Do you think she went back to the sea, Grandpa?"

"Oh yes. When a mermaid has once lost her magic garment you can be sure she will put it on again as soon as she can, to test it in the sea."

"Dad never told me this story," Ailsa thought as she and Grandpa went hand in hand back to the cottage.

The others were up and eating their breakfast. "Early birds!" said Mum.

Dad looked at Ailsa and Grandpa. "Did you have a walk, then?"

"No ..." said Ailsa.

"How about some breakfast?" said Grandpa.

That evening, when Dad came up to read a story at bedtime, they got talking instead.

"Grandad was sad today," Ailsa said.

"I know he sometimes is," said Dad. "What did he say?"

"He told me about Granny."

"Oh?" Dad sounded really surprised.

"Yes — how she found her magic garment again and went back to her home in the sea."

"That's what he said?"

"He was very upset. He was crying, Dad. Why did you tell her about the magic garment in the thatch? She would have stayed if she hadn't found it!"

"It wasn't a magic garment, really. It was just an old petticoat stuffed in rat hole in the thatch, to keep the draughts out."

"It was a magic garment. Grandpa said!" Ailsa felt like crying herself.

"I know. I've heard him tell that story too."

"But it was blue as the blue of the sea, green as the green of the seaweed, gold as the gold of the sand of the shore and it gleamed in his hand like a fish."

Dad put his arm round Ailsa. "Ailsa, Grandpa likes that story. It helps him to bear the pain."

"What pain?"

"The pain of Granny leaving him, leaving us."

"Where did she go then?"

"We never really knew for sure. One night, after she had bathed us and put us to bed, she must have packed her bag and left in the dark. I never saw her again."

"Didn't you miss her?"

"I'm sure we did. But it was a very long time ago, wasn't it?"

He gave Ailsa a big hug. "Time to sleep now. Tomorrow's another day," he whispered as he tucked her in.

Ailsa lay in the dark, thinking about her Grandpa and her unknown Granny. Which was the true story? Her own mum would *never* leave her and Dad. Would she?

Later that night, Ailsa woke up. The sound of the waves was overlaid with the light tapping of rain on the window panes. She went to the window and pulled back the curtain.

She followed with her eyes, as far as she could, the path that led down to the beach. It dipped out of sight and then, beyond it. She could see the top of the big flat picnic rock where she had sat with Grandpa. Was there someone sitting there now? She couldn't be certain. She opened the window and lent out. Yes — it was the mermaid! Ailsa felt sure she could see her pale face turned towards the cottage and she wondered if, like Grandpa, the mermaide had tears in her eyes.

Jean Dunning

BIBLIOGRAPHY

Aardema, Verna *Bimwili and the Zimwi* , Hamish Hamilton, 1986

Adams, Jeff *The Conspiracy of the Text*, RKP, 1986

Becker, A L 'Language in particular: a lecture' in Tannen, Deborah, ed. *Linguistics in Context: Connecting Observation and Understanding*, Ablex, 1988

Benjamin, Walter *Illuminations*, Fontana, 1970

Bettelheim, Bruno *The Uses of Enchantment*, Peregrine Books, 1976

Bruner, Jerome *Actual Minds, Possible Worlds*, Harvard University Press, 1986

Calvino, Italo, ed. *Italian Folk Stories*, Penguin 1987

Garvie, Edie *Story as Vehicle*, Multilingual Matters, 1990

Glassie, Henry, ed. *Irish Folk Tales*, Penguin, 1987

Heaney, Seamus 'The Fisherman and the Mermaid' in Rosen and Griffiths, eds. *That'd be Telling*, CUP, 1988

Heaney, Seamus 'Maighdean Mara' in *Wintering Out*, Faber, 1972

Hoggart, Richard *A Sort of Clowning: Life and Times; 1940-59*, Chatto & Windus, 1990

Holquist, M 'Answering as authoring. Mikhail Bakhtin's translinguistics' in *Critical Inquiry*, 10.2.83

Hunter, Ian *Memory*, Penguin, 1957

Jones, Derek and Medlicott, Mary, eds. *By Word of Mouth*, Channel Four Television, 1990

Marquez, Gabriel Garcia *One Hundred Years of Solitude*, Picador, 1967